LOSE THE BAGGAGE, LOSE THE WEIGHT

LOSE THE BAGGAGE, LOSE THE WEIGHT

a woman-to-woman recipe for life

REVISED EDITION

by Lorna Stremcha

Lose the Baggage, Lose the Weight
Copyright ©2013 by Lorna Stremcha. All rights reserved.

No part of this publication may be reproduced, stored in a retrieval system, or transmitted, in any form or by any means, electronic, mechanical, photocopying, recording, or otherwise, without prior written permission of the publisher.

Published by Resolutions! Media (Havre, MT)
www.lornastremcha.com
Cover and interior design by Blue Bull Book Design (bluebullbookdesign.com)

ISBN Soft Cover: 978-0-9913099-0-0
ISBN E-book (Kindle): 978-0-9913099-1-7
ISBN E-book (epub): 978-0-9913099-2-4

Printed and bound in the United States of America.

Originally published by Resolutions!: 2004
Published by Tate Publishing & Enterprises, LLC 2011
First Mass Market Printing: 2011

Library of Congress Cataloging-in-Publication Data

Stremcha, Lorna
Lose the Baggage; Lose the Weight a woman-to-woman recipe for life by Lorna Stremcha
1. Personal Growth/Self-Help/General 2. Health & Wellness/Women's Health 3. Psychology 4. Sociology 5. Creative Nonfiction

DISCLAIMER

This book does not seek to recommend any particular course of action, but rather share what the author has learned from her journey. The book does not constitute authority of law, but rather offers insight and strategies you might consider should you not be an expert.

*People who have experienced abuse and bullying may wish to seek support at the time of the reading due to the unpleasant memories that it may evoke.

Dedication

To *you* in hopes that *you* find *your* purposeful journey so you may live a life of wellness and joy.

Acknowledgements

To my family and friends who helped me along life's journey.

Author's Notes

Lose the Baggage, Lose the Weight is written with love, thoughtfulness, and an acquired purpose. Life has dealt me some hard knocks. And with hard knocks come life lessons. I whole-heartedly believe lessons taught are meant to be shared. Fortunately, I have the ability to do just that.

As a child while in the midst of chaos, I found refuge under the covers and in school. As a teen, life got more complicated; it led me to a hometown drug store in Livingston, Montana where I picked out a special Hallmark® card. In this card, I wrote a letter that ultimately helped shape me.

Mindful of that letter and grateful for every experience and person that has helped shape and mentor me, I share some of what I learned so you too may live a P.I.E.S. life—a life of physical, intellectual, emotional, and spiritual balance. Opportunities can help you see your hard knocks differently and can open the door to positive change.

* Your health and well-being are important to me. Before you start any diet or exercise program, please consult your doctor or healthcare professional.

Table of Contents

	Introduction	1
ONE:	First Steps	9
TWO:	Strategies, Techniques, & Visualization	31
THREE:	Bullies, Abusers, & Weight Issues	57
FOUR:	Overcoming the Bully Within	67
FIVE:	Gratitude, Attitude, & You	79
SIX:	Commitment, Promises, & Pledges	109
SEVEN:	Change	133
EIGHT:	Emotional Baggage	163
NINE:	Simply Put, Knowledge Is Power	205
TEN:	P.I.E.S & Diet Programs	239
ELEVEN:	Moving Forward & Lightening the Load	253
TWELVE:	Wrap It Up	289
	Weight Loss Grocery List	303
	Bibliography	309

Introduction

"The life which is unexamined is not worth living."
—Socrates

I believe in being totally honest. So let's begin.

My mother Doris was the little girl nobody wanted. At least, that's what she believed. She was married four times. Every time a subsequent marriage failed, she returned to her first husband, my father. Each marriage was the same nightmare of abuse and addiction.

I was raped at a very young age and abused at different times in my life. My brothers, sister and I lived in poverty. While in the midst of this chaos, we experienced life as wards of the State of Montana, and our mother spent time in Montana's state mental institution. She fought the courts to get us back. Eventually, we were returned to our mother only to face the same abuse and addiction. I stayed with her until my junior year in high school.

When I couldn't take it any longer, I left a Hallmark® card with a short note of good-bye on the kitchen table and went into hiding. That was me at seventeen. *At risk* was the official term to describe me. At risk and set up for a lifetime of sadness, of failure.

Despite such a gloomy prognosis, my life did not develop that way, nor have I ever seen my life in that light.

How did I beat the odds?

I focused on the things I could control and accepted the things beyond my control. I believed in myself even when others didn't and listened to those that believed in me. I developed self-honesty and examined my life even when it hurt. I prayed every day and found ways to master my skills. I realized if I wanted to achieve certain goals I needed plans and ways to execute those plans. Understanding that the life I was born into was one of chaos, I purposely sought out positive role models.

From a very young age, I befriended peers who were healthy, happy, and living in safe and productive environments with parents or guardians that nurtured them. I studied their families' actions and behaviors. I talked with their parents and absorbed any advice they were willing to share. My heart would break when my friends would shout hurtful words at their parents and throw temper tantrums just because they didn't get their way or what they wanted. Their entitled attitude bothered me almost as much as I longed for the life they lived.

Being naturally optimistic, I quickly learned the value of dumping negatives and stock piling positives. I took inventory of those with bad practices and self-destructive traits. Life showed me how cruel it could be if I choose to ignore its lessons.

Instead of dwelling on how bad life was I approached it with the attitude that others had it much worse. I believed with all my heart God had a very special plan for my life, but it was up to me to implement it. I strategized and developed ways to get from point A to point B— ultimately to point C. This required; belief, focus, drive, motivation, flexibility, acceptance, a heck of a lot of pain, patience, and gratitude.

My life demanded that I break through barriers that stood in my way. It showed me how challenges are oftentimes opportunities cloaked as obstacles. More importantly, it provided me with compassion, common sense, a fighting spirit sprinkled with a bit of stubbornness and a great amount of empathy.

With that said, please keep in mind everyone's journey is different. A less traveled path can also be very enlightening.

Let's learn about P.I.E.S.

How I Created P.I.E.S.

I first began sharing my ideas about personal development in the early 1980s working with The Miss Montana Road Show. This educational program, affiliated with the Miss America pageant, featured Miss Montana, selected finalists and other performers. My role was to motivate and inspire audiences, primarily adolescents to embrace individuality—the importance of you. I continue to work with the Miss Montana/Miss America program today.

After college, I began a career in Portland, Oregon. Here, I developed what I called my "Ingredients for Success". The title made sense, for as a weight loss counselor/manager and personal trainer, I was accustomed to showing clients how to measure and weigh their food, as well as their bodies.

During this time, I learned there was much more to wellness and fitness than grocery lists and a scale. Instead of a recipe for food, I decided to create a recipe for a person. I thought about what was universal and made me, myself whole. *Think food.*

I took an everyday measuring cup and mentally divided it by fourths: one quarter, physical; the second, intellectual; the third, emotional; the fourth and perhaps the most important, spiritual. When you put these four pieces together holistically, you have an evenly balanced individual. *Simple.*

At this time, I was called to work with high school girls at risk facing many of the many pitfalls I had circumvented. Sharing my personal story allowed me to introduce the following concepts to these young women:

- Your past is no excuse for your future
- The power within
- Goal setting
- Choices and consequences

- Be true to you, individuality
- Complete your education and graduate from high school. Think about a secondary education.

As you can see, I was teaching the basic principles of P.I.E.S.: self-advocacy, self-esteem, self-image, nutrition, fitness, and goal setting.

In the mid-1980s, along with two other women from the Portland, Oregon, area I started a part-time business, Self-Image 85. This business followed the same basic principles, fitness now, nutrition, self-esteem, and wardrobe and makeup.

After leaving Oregon, I moved back to Montana and continued to present workshops and direct programs following the same basic formula. Common threads have always remained at the center of each of my career choices and volunteer work: women and girls in need; life skill lessons; the power of you; nutrition and fitness; the value of education and the importance of creativity and vision.

I did not title my philosophy P.I.E.S. until 2002 when a friend of mine, a therapist, showed my material to her husband. In that document, I had listed the words physical, intellectual, emotional, and spiritual with definitions. Each word was a quarter of a pie graph representing the parts which make up a whole person.

"This spells pies," said my friend's husband.

That was my "A ha!" moment.

P.I.E.S. philosophy was born.

P.I.E.S. Philosophy

Physical is a state of well-being. To achieve bodily wellness and maintain it once it is achieved, it is necessary to feed the body with nutritious foods, exercise it regularly, avoid harmful behaviors and substances, and protect one's self from accidents or harm.

Intellectual is the ability to think and learn from life's experiences, both taught to us and experienced by us. It is a willingness to be open-minded to new ideas, and the ability to question and evaluate information with reason and logic. An individual with good intellectual skills is capable of making decisions, setting realistic goals, meeting challenges, and coming up with sensible and practical solutions to their problems.

Emotional is the ability to differentiate thoughts and feelings and to communicate them reasonably and responsibly. It is the ability to interact effectively with other people in social environments. It is the capacity to develop satisfying interpersonal relationships and to fulfill social and workplace roles.

Spiritual is a belief in a higher power that gives greater significance to individual life.

P.I.E.S. Purpose

I refer to knowledge acquired throughout the years as taking a P.I.E.S. journey. The purpose of P.I.E.S. is to help *you* live a more harmonious and balanced life: physically, intellectually, emotionally, and spiritually. Other intended purposes include developing: self-awareness, self-confidence, self-image, self-esteem, self-management, self-reliance, awareness of others and their needs. P.I.E.S.'s ultimate purpose is to help you create positive and healthy changes daily. And to help *you* realize *your* successes come from within *you*.

    Desire
+ Motivation
+ Commitment
+ Flexibility
+ <u>Acceptance</u>
= Change

About This Book

This book is written for *you*.

It is a book of self-discovery intended to be engaging and interactive. The primary purpose is to help you gain a better understanding of your needs and wants.

Throughout the book, you will be asked questions that require simple yes or no answers. You will be asked to write your thoughts down. Feel free to write in the margins. This is a book to be used, not kept on a shelf. Some of these questions may be difficult and emotional. What I ask of *you*, I have asked of myself.

Your goal is not to be perfect.

When *you* participate in a lesson, it is important you respond with honesty and articulate your thoughts or ideas as clearly as possible. This will help you gain clarity and focus so you can begin to live a P.I.E.S. life.

Writing helps us to generate ideas, create plans, translate thoughts, revise thoughts and evaluate the effectiveness of our thoughts.

To help with your journey, you will come across a variety of voices brave enough to share their experiences. At times the stories and lessons may be disturbing, but read on, for they offer hope.

You will also come across narrative writings referred to as *A Piece of Me*, where I reveal events, circumstances, and experiences that have affected my life. In addition, I have included some of my favorite and most meaningful quotes, prayers and poetry.

It is my hope that these writings and lessons will also help you to develop better critical thinking and reasoning skills, become a better problem-solver and help you to gain a better understanding about others and your surroundings.

Each chapter includes lessons with a specific topic. Chapters begin with *Something to Think About* accompanied by a favorite quote, a place to log the date, and a signature line. Chapters end with *Data Dump* where I have provided you with a place to ask for forgiveness and forgive yourself. This is to help you unload and/or offer thoughts or revelations from the day. I have also included appropriate word banks where needed.

"People with good spiritual health identify their own basic purpose in life; learn how to experience love, joy, peace, and fulfillment; and help themselves and others achieve their full potential. They concern themselves with giving, forgiving, and attending to others' needs before one's own needs."
—Roger Smith, Michigan State University

Chapter One

First Steps

Something to think about:

"A journey of a thousand miles begins with a single step."
—Lao-tzu

Date: _____
Today, I give thanks for

Signature: _____

Successful journeys begin with first steps and the willingness to change and/or grow: physically, intellectually, emotionally, and spiritually. Each step requires consistent focus and action.

Self-discovery is part of this process and demands honesty. This can be painful and uncomfortable; however without truthfulness *you* gain nothing. Without facts, it is difficult to move from where *you* are to where *you* want to go. Achievements require plans. Plans help *you* move forward. *Understanding self-advocacy, self-care, self-esteem, and self-image are key components to self-discovery.*

Self-advocacy requires *you* work on *your* own behalf and understand and articulate *your* needs and wants to others. Self-advocacy requires self-worthiness and self-love. Self-care is to care for *you*. To have self-esteem is to think well of yourself and to give yourself respect. Self-image is to have a conception of *your* abilities, ambitions, and idea of *your* true or authentic self.

Standing up for *your* legal and personal rights can be overwhelming and intimidating, especially when exposed to toxic environments and people. Those who experience abandonment, abuse, addiction, bullying, loss, rape or have weight or other significant health issues may find self-advocacy difficult.

Self-advocacy takes effort, time, and courage. Advocating on your own behalf can lead to uncomfortable and painful feelings and experiences which can be frightening and sometimes dangerous. Therefore, I highly recommend discussing your concerns with a professional.

Change becomes problematic when *you* are conditioned to put *your* needs and wants second. This behavior can often be generational and unintentionally modeled. Witnessing *your* mother or another female mentor succumb to subservience devalues *your* own needs and wants. Observing role models physically beaten or verbally/or emotionally abused can result in mimicking behavior.

Many of us have been conditioned to believe putting our needs first is selfish. We often feel shamefulness and guilt when we do. When self-advocacy is lacking low self-esteem, poor self-image, depression, weight issues, work issues, domestic issues, and other issues can develop.

Demi's Dilemma

Demi, blonde haired, blue-eyed and still beautiful in her 50s, is a long-time friend who lacks self-esteem. She entered the world eleven months after her sister, Mary. As a child, Demi's father beat her with a belt, leaving welts and bruises. Her mother shamed her with hurtful words and her grandfather sexually abused her. Mary mimicked the family's abusive behavior and bullied Demi.

At age eighteen, Demi's parents kicked her out of their house and out on her own. With only a few belongings, she walked onto a small Montana college campus. Here Demi began a new life, earning a degree in Elementary Education. Shortly after graduation, she entered the world of work in her chosen profession. Demi became a successful tenured teacher, then a victim of sexual assault by her principal. Upon reporting the incident, Demi was accused of being the abuser, professionally humiliated, suspended and then terminated. (It is important to note Demi's experience is unfortunately too common in sexual harassment/hostile workplace scenarios where the abuser reverses charges and remains unpunished).

With no support and unable to find a teaching position in Montana, Demi packed up her two young children and moved out of state.

Eleven years later, as an empty nester, Demi hit rock bottom. Fifty pounds overweight and in another abusive relationship, she made the courageous decision to leave. Demi returned to her parent's home with hope of reconnecting and mending broken relationships. *The desire for reconciliation must be mutual. Without that all your efforts are futile.*

Unable to change her parent's treatment of her, or find work in her hometown, Demi relocated. With a fresh start in a new community, she found herself in yet another abusive situation. This time Demi found the strength to walk away.

Weeks later, Demi secured a job as a paraprofessional and moved in with a longtime friend. Still desperately longing to heal the relationship with her parents, Demi returned home for a visit, only to be rejected again. *You cannot bury your past. It's just that simple.*

Demi had been silent and ashamed about her past for more than three decades. I knew she was going through a rough time and in a fragile state. Her last attempt at reconciliation with her family caused her to finally reveal her deeply hidden secrets.

"What are you trying to accomplish? " I asked.

"I moved back home to be around family and put my life back together. And all I hear is 'you are crap' from my father and 'you can't do anything from my mother'. Others tell me my life is a mess because I don't live a God-fearing life. I'm religious; I am just not a fundamentalist and fanatic," she told me.

"Have you ever shared your story with a counselor, therapist or psychologist?" I asked.

"No," she replied.

"You need to let others help you, and that may mean getting professional help," I told her.

Is it any wonder that Demi lost self-worth and forgot how to care for herself? She needs someone to advocate for her, so she can learn to advocate for herself. Demi must make some challenging changes and also remove negative stressors from her life.

I know this is hard, but it is necessary to understand your past before you can begin the process of healing. This is all part of the P.I.E.S. journey.

Angela's Challenge

Angela, 23, a young acquaintance, started college three months after high school. Growing up, she spent many hours alone while her single mother worked late and partied on weekends. Most Sundays, Angela awoke to a visiting stranger and a hung over mother. Many times, the weekend drinking binges extended through Sunday night, leading to another hangover on Monday. Angela's mother often requested her daughter call her in sick to work. This put Angela in the parental driver's seat, allowing the high school student to come and go as she pleased and play hooky on occasion.

When Angela started college, she patterned her mother's risky behavior, resulting in hangovers. She also began skipping class and was placed on academic probation. In addition to drinking and partying, midway into her freshman year, Angela's boyfriend broke up with her. Her emotions spiraled out of control, leading to promiscuity and sexual experimentation. She entered into abusive relationships. Needless to say, her self-care, self-esteem and self-image, soon hit bottom and she felt alone and abandoned. Angela sought out any attention she could get. Unfortunately, this resulted in a plot to become pregnant with an abusive partner. *How can Angela break the pattern of abusive behavior for herself and her child?*

Purposeful Parenting

"The purpose of parenting is to protect and prepare children to survive and thrive in the kind of society in which they live," states parenting expert Michael Popkin, Ph.D. This vital purpose was lost in both Demi and Angela's lives and they suffered. *Do you want to survive or thrive?*

- To thrive means to get the most out of life and to grow and develop well.
- To survive means to endure or to sustain the effects of and continue to live. (to just get by)

For Demi and Angela and other women like them, there is opportunity for change and growth but it will take effort, patience and time.

How do *you* learn self-care, develop self-esteem and self-image if the most important female(s) in your life do not model it?

This is a fact. You cannot change anyone but yourself. You control you. The question is "are *you* willing to put in the time it takes to develop positive traits?"

Like a child who experiences nature for the very first time *you* must be willing to see your world differently. You must build a team who will support: action, accountability, belief, courage, drive, cooperation, honesty, focus, interpersonal communication skills, decision making skills, mutual respect and responsibility to help you step out of the victim role into the survivor role.

Before beginning your self-discovery journey you must be willing to be your own advocate. I cannot stress this enough. You must want to take on the challenge of change. Transformation can be painful, because it requires brutal honesty — a task difficult for most of us. Pain is a great motivator. When we are hurting: physically, intellectually, emotionally, or spiritually we want the pain to go away.

Mindful change begins when *you* identify the problem or problems and stop the excuses, justifications, and rationalizations. You must familiarize yourself with *your* issues and stop comparing yourself to others. *You* must associate with people *you* most want to be like.

$$Drive + Focus + Action = Change$$

Here are some healthy reminders to help *you* get on track:

- Wise people learn from other's mistakes and fools learn from their own.
- You own your problems.
- All people have problems. Successful people handle their problems.
- All families have problems. Successful families handle their problems.
- We all (families too) work at our own pace.
- Associate with successful people.
- Communication is the key to success.
- Change is not easy for anybody.
- Sometimes it is necessary to get professional help.

> "Mentoring isn't a discussion. It's an obligation."
> —Gail Evans, author of *Play Like a Man, Win Like a Woman*

Switch the Channel

To achieve success switch to Channel Positive. You must recondition and take better care of yourself. Understand self-care is not selfish! Doing enjoyable and healthy activities will not hurt anyone. Taking fifteen minutes out of *your* busy day to relax is okay. Wellness routines are beneficial to *you* and those linked to you. Self-care means to value *you* and there is absolutely nothing wrong with that. *When you value yourself, you channel the Survivor within you.*

With this new role comes empowerment. You are more aware of your surroundings and begin to understand personal, professional and sociological responsibility. Breaking patterns of negative behaviors takes courage and knowledge—especially if *you* were a victim yourself. Positive risk taking, self-advocacy, self-confidence, self-esteem and self- image are tools needed to break the cycle of negative behavior passed from generation to generation. Poor decision making is another result of the abuse cycle. Assertiveness skills also fall short.

Keep in mind, an advocate or mentor who works on your behalf can help. A mentor will coach you, stand beside you, and help you become stronger. As a result, you will become empowered.

Positive mentors promote: healthy life skills, problem solving skills, interpersonal communication skills, focus, motivation, moral support, guidance, leadership skills, sportsmanship skills, positive and objective feedback, academic discipline routines, self-management skills, cultural and spiritual awareness, and volunteerism skills.

Positive mentees must be: accepting, flexible, willing learners, ask questions, communicate openly, exhibit positive conduct and take personal responsibility seriously. *When you are inspired by women with healthy self-images and self-esteem you yourself become inspiring.* Following the Principals of P.I.E.S. produces stronger and healthier bodies, healthier homes, healthier work places, and healthier communities.

Refuel

"Energy is never lost, only misplaced."

—Angel Wisdom

Imagine your body as liquid energy. Throughout the day you are asked to give your energy to your spouse, children, siblings, friends, students, patients, coworkers, job, home, charity or club. By the end of the day you are empty. *This is not good for you.*

Professionals in the fields of nursing, teaching, and social work often need to refuel before the end of the day. Their gauge was probably low within the first few hours of work. This is because individuals that are drawn to these professions are more concerned about needs of others more than their own.

As an educator and Life Coach, I can attest to the fact a dedicated professional's day begins early in the morning and more often than not, ends late at night. The moment a teacher arrives at school, demands are made. Dedicated teachers have little time for themselves. They do much more than simply teach their subject. Many students do not have positive role models at home; it falls upon the teacher to provide guidance and monitoring. Most teachers have counseled, tutored, broken up a fight, refereed an argument, attended a couple conferences and taught three classes, all before lunch.

Granted, most are content and do not complain. They love their students and enjoy teaching. Dedicated teachers inspire, develop and educate. As with other service field professions, such as nursing and social work, the day is consumed meeting others demands and neglecting their own.

Is your energy gauge on empty? If so, you need to refuel and become self-caring and *your* own best advocate.

Are your past beliefs and behaviors getting in your way? Experiences, negative or positive determine how you handle situations. You must also understand your perception affects how you view yourself and others. Personal beliefs and learned behavior often get in the way of success.

An example: "I failed at this already. I'm sure to fail again." To believe just because you failed the first time you are doomed to fail the next, is self-defeating. Failure is often the best thing that can happen to us.

Many people refuse to compete because they are afraid of losing. You can't lose if you don't compete! Competition provides the opportunity to learn more in a compressed time-frame. This can be applied to every aspect of your life: workouts, wellness routines, clubs, hobbies and academics. *Remember, you are really only competing against yourself, not others.*

For many of us, just getting through the day is winning. Women and girls subjected to abuse, abandonment, or addiction have been coerced into silence, brainwashed into self-abuse, and trapped in an environment that keeps them chained to beliefs that they are stupid, a loser, a fool, ugly, fat, a tramp, or worthless. Their distorted view of themselves prevents them from getting back up and standing on their own two feet. *Are false perceptions and negative feedback shattering your spirit?*

EXERCISE: *Four Action Steps*

Circle one step from each section.
1. Get moving.
    a. Walk, dance, swim, etc...
    b. Practice breath-walking (www.breathwalk.com)
    c. Commit out loud.
2. Charge up your brain.
    a. Read
    b. Listen to a webinar
    c. Research
3. Choose a positive emotion.
    a. Smile
    b. Gratitude
    c. Banish negative words.
4. Spiritual
    a. Pray
    b. Meditate
    c. Visualize

What four things in each category did you commit to and what actions did you take? Use one or two feeling words to describe how that action made you feel. Be specific. Example: Walking for ½ hour made me feel invigorated.

1.

2.

3.

4.

EXERCISE: *Dumping Negative Stressors*

Write down four unimportant stressors and express how that stressor makes you feel. Then write a solution. Example: I don't like being late for work or school because it makes feel irresponsible.

Stressor: late for work/school
Feeling: irresponsible
Solution: I can solve this problem by going to bed earlier and getting up earlier in the morning.

1.

2.

3.

4.

EXERCISE: *Vocabulary Review*

Fill in the blank. (self-care, self-advocate, self-esteem, advocate, self-image)

1. To _____ for someone is to act on someone's behalf.
2. To be a _____ is to act on your own behalf.
3. To think well of one's self and to give one self- respect is _____.
4. To have a conception of one's self, abilities, ambitions and idea of true or authentic-self.
5. To care for yourself is _____.

Check your answers:

1. advocate
2. self-advocate
3. self-esteem
4. self- image
5. self-care

EXERCISE: *Self*

Answer these questions:

Do you like yourself? Yes or No

Do you think you are a good human being? Yes or No

Do you believe you deserve love? Yes or No

Do you believe you deserve happiness? Yes or No

Do you feel you are good person? Yes or No

Are your unspoken thoughts and feelings affecting you negatively or positively? Explain

What one thing can you change today? Explain

Self-Esteem

People with shattered spirits find it difficult to answer *yes* to these questions. Did you find it difficult to answer *yes*? Don't despair; there is hope. That's why I wrote this book. Developing a healthy self-esteem allows you to create the life you desire and cope with life's challenges.

Simply put, low self-esteem creates problems. It can make you feel anxious, stressed, lonely, and depressed. It also can cause relationship issues: family, friends, and intimate partners. Low self-esteem creates academic, career, and job-related problems. It can lead to alcohol, drug, and eating problems. Low self-esteem makes for unhappy and nonproductive people. *When you look in your emotional mirror, what are the traits you see?*

EXERCISE: *Reflections*

Put a check mark beside each trait that fits you.

___I am unworthy of love and affection.

___I fear rejection.

___I feel like an outcast in my community (family, church, profession).

___I feel like a failure.

___I feel isolated from the outside world.

___I feel abused when faced with constructive criticism.

___I am in constant pain and vulnerable to emotional attacks.

If you checked more than three, we have work to do. It won't be easy. But if *you* are honest with yourself, *you* should make progress. *Have you become a master of avoidance?*

EXERCISE: *Avoidance*

Do you avoid thoughts, feelings, or conversations that remind you of your abusers, your perceived failures? Yes or No

Do you purposely avoid activities, people, or places that remind you of your abuse or perceived failures? Yes or No

Do you have a difficult time remembering important parts of your abuse or perceived failures? Yes or No

Sometimes avoidance is a good thing. It helps protect you. But it can also harm you. Thankfully, I am able to share what rescued me and offer you strategies. I can show you hopeful moments, suggest guidance, and provide P.I.E.S. teachings and wisdom.

I am acquainted with the physical and emotional damage of negative self-talk. The anguish of releasing the secrets and the accompanying pain is frightening. I get that. However, I have experienced pain turned to joy, darkness turned to light, and nightmares turned to hope and promise.

> "We think sometimes that poverty is only being hungry, naked, and homeless. The poverty of being unwanted, unloved, and uncared for is the greatest poverty. We must start in our own homes to remedy this kind of poverty."
> —Mother Teresa

A PIECE OF ME

Filling the Void

We share the need to be wanted. It's human nature. So when we are feeling unwanted or empty, we often seek out ways to fill that emptiness. In the 1960s, my mom disappeared with the carnival. She had an array of reasons for taking such action. She was unbalanced emotionally. She felt her life was out of control. It probably was.

    She was in her early twenties, with four children and a husband. She had just given birth to a gravely ill child, who was fathered by another man. She was keeping this a secret. She was forced to move to the state of Washington so the new baby could be cared for at a Tacoma hospital. Her father was dying of cancer in Livingston, Montana. She was a victim of rape. One of her children had been raped. Her life was out of control. She was overwhelmed with shame, guilt, anger, confusion, mistrust, and hopelessness. She wanted to be rid of her problems. She wanted to disappear. Like the cancerous tumor that was cut from her papa's eye, she wanted to remove the ugly problems in her life. She was overcome with despair and loss.

    She wanted to fill her emptiness and erase her mistakes. So, instead of seeking help to gain emotional balance or control, she literally walked away with the carnival. She escaped.

    Having your mother abandon you makes you feel alone, lost, and empty. It tends to create a fear and emptiness, which is difficult to fill. Like my mother, many people try to fill these voids. They use sex, alcohol, food, and things to try to fill them up. However, they find that sex, alcohol, food, and things cannot fill a void.

This is a feeling we must learn to fill ourselves. I am not saying it is easy. Mothers are supposed to be there for us. A mother is that one person we are supposed to be able to count on no matter what the circumstance. Mothers aren't supposed to just walk away and leave. People are not supposed to violate us, and it is difficult when someone dies. However, sometimes we are given gifts that help us fill these voids; it is just that we cannot always see clearly.

Even though my mother left with the carnies, life in Whitehall wasn't all that bad; for it was during this time I bonded with my Grandpa and Grandma Parsons. Fishing and camping were regular pastimes for the Parsons clan. They were born fishermen—every one of them.

When Grandpa Parsons fished the Gallatin, Madison, and Missouri, I watched with joy as he stood in the middle of his chosen river tossing his pole. Watching Grandpa fish was like watching a ballet on the water. His toss was gentle, and when the wind caught hold of the fishing line, it danced. Then it would merge gracefully with the water with the slightest splash. Watching Grandpa fish gave me great pleasure. It filled me up.

Though Mom had walked away and emptiness inside of me existed, I never obsessed over her disappearance because I knew I was loved. Grandpa showed me he loved me, just as he had shown the grandchildren before me and his children before them. The whispers of nature, God, the angels, and my grandfather were able to help fill that void. He showed me it was my choice to fill that void. It could not be filled by anybody else but me. Ultimately, I knew my mother loved me because she left me in good hands.

And because it is human nature to want to hold on to something tangible, to help fill this need, my daddy saw to it that Santa delivered a Thumbelina doll to me for Christmas the year my mom joined the carnival. It, too, helped fill that void of emptiness. For my overwhelming connection had nothing to do with possessing a doll but wanting desperately to feel needed and wanted.

I knew the fairy tale of Thumbelina; Daddy, Grandpa, and Grandma did too. So in their wisdom, they gifted me a tiny doll-child that I wanted, that I needed to fill the void that left me hungry and aching. For I knew that Thumbelina was wanted more than anything, and when my loved ones gave me a doll with such significance, they realized that I would feel the power of being deeply loved; my spirit would be freed.

EXERCISE: *Emptiness*

Do you feel empty? Yes or No

Did someone in your life ever try to fill your void, your emptiness? Yes or No

If so, who?

Did any object help fill that void? Yes or No

If so, what?

Did you lose a mother, a father, a friend, or a grandparent that created emptiness?

If so, how did that affect you? Explain

Were you abandoned? Yes or No

Do you still feel abandoned? Yes or No

What makes you feel that way? Explain

Were you abused, raped, or violated? Yes or No

Did you lose something, and do you feel that empty panging of hunger? Yes or No

Did you have to learn to mask your feelings just to get by? Yes or No

Did you have to eat and eat and eat just to try to fill that emptiness? Yes or No

Did you marry just to marry, not because you were in love, but to fill a void? Yes or No

Did you have sex to fill a void? Yes or No

Did you try to starve yourself to avoid your problems, your pain? Yes or No

Did you starve to make the problem disappear, only to find it never went away? Yes or No

Did you bury your box full of stuff so deeply that when it opened it exploded like Mount St. Helens? Yes or No

Did you have a grandparent, a friend, a mentor, a doctor, or anyone that was willing to let you explode, release your emotions, fill your emptiness, or acknowledge your fears? Yes or No

Did you have a way to escape? Yes or No

DATA DUMP

Please forgive me for:

I forgive myself for:

P.I.E.S. Reminder

"You are the only you God made... God made you and broke the mold."

— Max Lucado

Chapter Two

Strategies, Techniques, & Visualization

Something to think about:

> "I find refuge under the covers, because I can. It isn't always smart to hide, but sometimes I just have to."
> —Lorna (Parsons) Stremcha

Date: _____
Today, I give thanks for

Signature: _____

A PIECE OF ME

Clouds & Linen

Now I lay me down to sleep;
I pray the Lord my soul to keep.
If I should die before I wake,
I pray the Lord my soul to take.

For as long as I can remember, every time something bothered me, terrified me, or overwhelmed me, I would go to my safe place under the covers. I would pray. I would close my eyes and pray. From there, I would take a journey to the blue sky where one soft, white, fluffy cumulus cloud waited for me. On that cumulus cloud rested a brass bed with clean white linens and a fluffy white-feathered comforter. I would repeat over and over again, "This is just a bad dream. This is just a bad dream. When I wake up, everything will be better." I then would fall fast asleep, resting in heaven with a smile.

My dream became my reality. If only for a few brief minutes, it became my reality. It became my peace. It was my way of escaping, my way of coping with all the confusion, violence, abandonment, and fear. It provided me the ability to move on. It was my way of me protecting me.

To this day, there are times I lay in bed under the covers when I am afraid. Curling up on my bed seems safe. It is as if the rest of the world cannot touch me. That's a ridiculous way of thinking; nonetheless, that's my way of thinking. Childish, I know. It's my escape. My safe place. I'm pleased that I learned this skill of avoidance. Without it and my belief in God, I fear I would have gone so deep inside myself that I would have never awakened.

EXERCISE: *Strategies*

Thankfully, I have picked up healthier strategies and techniques since childhood. Strategies that help me face my fears, gain control of my emotions, and relax are:

- Ducky Float
- Grab the Furniture
- A Day at the Ocean
- Basic Relaxation/Visualization

DUCKY FLOAT

Proper belly breathing increases the flow of oxygen and has a calming effect on the mind and body. To check if you are breathing properly, lie on your back and put a rubber ducky or favorite toy on your abdomen. The duck, not your chest, should float up and down. Sometimes simple things can make a difference. Watch the ducky for a while.

GRAB THE FURNITURE

The other is a grounding exercise given to me by a mental health expert. It is divided into four steps. I found this particular exercise to be helpful when feeling unsafe.

Grounding: Grab furniture with hands, open eyes and observe your location now.

Say to self: My name is _____. I am _____ years old. Today is _____. And I am at _____ (name the exact location). I am safe; I am not back in the place where they _____ and _____ me. I am not as vulnerable as I was, and the _____ is not happening now.

Repeat this until you are calm. Do this ten times a day if you need to.

A DAY AT THE OCEAN

I am on the Oregon beach walking. The beach is huge and goes and goes. I can hear the sound of the waves. It is calm today, not crashing, and the sky's blue. The sun is shining down on my head, and the sand is warm under my feet. I'm walking barefoot, and the sand is white and gritty. I walk along looking down at the seashells and the glistening sand where the tide has gone out. I hear the seagulls overhead. The temperature is just perfect. It's about eighty-eight degrees. The sun feels hot; there is a light sea breeze. The smell of the ocean air is full of seaweed and sand. It smells good. To my left, the waves are breaking against the rocks. I walk into the surf up to my knees. Life is perfect. The day is perfect.

Today, create your safe place. Use your own location. It should be a favorite place with pleasant memories. In a quiet, private room, record your script and play it. If you want, add calm music (instrumental or sounds of the environment) that help taking you where you need to be. You can use mine if you like; just do this one unselfish task for yourself today.

BASIC RELAXATION/VISUALIZATION

- Cozy up on a comfortable chair.
- Wiggle your toes and adjust your feet, arms, and back so you are completely comfortable.
- Take deep breaths to release all the tension.
- Tighten your left hand into a fist; then let go until limp.
- Tighten your right hand into a fist; then let go until limp.
- Tense your leg muscles; then let go until limp.
- Force a grin on your face; then let go until your face feels relaxed and limp.
- Enjoy the feeling of being limp throughout your entire body. Feel the relaxed heaviness as it takes over your entire body. Remain relaxed and quiet. Hear and see only the breathing.
- With every breath you take, allow yourself to go deeper and deeper into a state of looseness, agelessness, and limpness.
- Let all thoughts escape your mind.
- After the mind is cleared, begin to visualize yourself enjoying your life (pain free).
- Picture yourself as healthy and happy, full of zest and vibrant energy.
- See yourself as you go into an even deeper state of relaxation. Tell yourself that on the count of three you will emerge from this quiet state feeling wonderful and full of energy.
- Count aloud: one, two, and three.
- You are awake and refreshed.

"Undoubtedly, we become what we envisage."
—Claude M. Bristol

A PIECE OF ME

A Sister's Lesson

It was the mid-1970s, and we were living in Livingston, Montana. My sister was visiting after emancipating herself. Her zestfulness and love of self was a lesson that will forever play as a fond memory. As a person who would later help others develop a healthy self-image, I found a valuable lesson in the way Dairene viewed herself. She expressed this love at the age of thirteen years old. Though I doubt she knew what she was doing at the time, it really is quite remarkable. So what exactly was she doing?

From my upstairs bedroom, I could hear a voice. I thought someone was visiting. The voice was happy and confident, so I veered downstairs and saw only Dairene. She was standing smiling and talking to herself in the mirror. I stood in amusement as I watched and listened. With great confidence, she was telling herself that she was *so* ... cute. She really was a petite cutie, but to tell yourself that struck me as absurd. Being the older sister, I thought Dairene to be conceited. I even called her on it. I really shouldn't have done that. I'll tell you why.

She was developing a healthy self-image; I could have destroyed that. Thank God I had the wherewithal to apologize and started practicing her method myself. However, I never used the word cute. I did speak about intelligence, talent, and yes, used the word pretty sparingly. I did feel ridiculous at first, but came to practice my sister's lesson often. Though I didn't always use the mirror, I did practice this method nightly, in meditation and prayer.

Living in a world of chaos, this practice gave me solace and hope. I recognize the lesson as one that helped me develop the confidence I needed to make difficult decisions. It is a lesson I continue to use today. Although the lesson seems simple and silly, it really does help with the reprogramming process. After all, who knows you better than you do? So why not have a little talk with your best friend or worst enemy to help create a better you? After all, you practice this in privacy.

It can be done in a quiet room where meditation is easy or in your own bathroom with the door closed in ultimate privacy. Then without realizing it, you try to improve yourself at the start of each new day; of course, you achieve quite a lot in the course of time. Anyone can do this; it costs nothing and is certainly very helpful.

Changing your way of thinking is hard work. For years you have been beating on yourself and feeding your mind with negativism; however, it can be done with diligence, practice, and a lot of patience. Here's a little exercise I want you to get started on today, at your convenience. You need to do this one every day. Sometimes, you need to do it many times a day.

EXERCISE: *Mirror Talk*

Need: One Mirror and You

- Stand in front of the mirror.
- Look at yourself in the mirror.
- Study yourself.
- Become the subject.
- Notice your posture, your demeanor.

- Role your shoulders back and stick out your chest.
- Smile. (Are you smiling yet? Come on, you can do it. There you go.)
- Say to yourself: I am _____, and I am beautiful and worthy of living a happy, prosperous, and healthy life full of love. (You do not have to follow my script; you can make up your own. Keep it positive, and mean it.)
- Repeat I am _____ six more times.
- Do this three times a day.

"Whatever you focus on you're going to believe. Focus equals reality to the individual, even though it's not reality in actuality."
—Anthony Robbins

A PIECE OF ME

A Bewitching Picture

Kissing a picture of Elizabeth Montgomery in her role as Serena cut from *Tiger Beat* magazine may seem silly. But I assure you if it were the only concrete possession you owned connecting you to your mother, you wouldn't see the humor in it at all.

While most of us remember Elizabeth in her title role of Samantha in *Bewitched*, we loved her when she played her cousin Serena. With the dark hair required for that role, the resemblance between my mother and Serena was uncanny. It was so real to my sister, Dairene, and me that we convinced ourselves that it was our mother. In truth, we knew it was not, but this distorted view of reality is what gave us solace. The bond we shared with this picture became so strong that we reported our daily happenings to it, treating it as it were our mother. With each one-sided conversation, we wishfully waited for a response. Out of faithfulness and trust, we confided our deepest thoughts and confessed our greatest sins to the picture that hung on the wall above the light switch. We spoke to it with such honesty that anyone who overheard us might think we were speaking to a Catholic priest during confessional.

Each passing day brought with it the heavy weight of burdens that rested on our small, narrow shoulders. However, because of the magic that the picture provided, the load seemed lighter and much easier to hold. The picture served its purpose well by allowing us to surrender our heartaches and problems. This eight-by-ten photograph taken by a stranger offered not only a smiling face to look at, but also a sense of belonging that only a foster child could understand.

We came to anticipate bedtime for it was our time with our mommy. In those minutes before sleep, we shared our frustrations, wishes, and joys with her as we lay in our twin beds and stared at her beautiful face before bedtime prayer. With God's watchful eye and mother's smiling face, we managed to muster a smile before falling fast asleep. Nightmares became less frequent. Most nights did not seem so dark because we knew morning would come; with it came hope.

So as the morning sun warmed the room, Elizabeth's smile greeted us and fueled us with the courage to face the day ahead. It was the only picture on the wall. Though it was just a picture to many who read *Tiger Beat*, it was our umbilical cord.

As time marched on, the picture became priceless. After all, it was literally the only connection we had with our mother. The welfare system and our foster parents forbade any form of communication with our parents and that meant even a photograph. Out of fear, the photograph remained a well-hidden secret. Out of necessity, we kept our secret from our two brothers because the last thing we wanted was for it to be ripped from the wall.

The gratitude my sister and I felt for the picture that hung in Aunt Mae's spare bedroom was immeasurable. The picture became like a shrine. We were careful not to tear it or smudge it in any way, for it and our devotion to God is what gave us hope. Montgomery's smiling face filled our room with grace and comfort; it provided us the opportunity to kiss our mommy good night and tell her we loved her.

Now as a woman, reflecting back to this time of my life, I can see with clarity that it was not by any means an accident or chance that we found this particular picture to hang on our bare wall. It was God and his angels working overtime to save two innocent souls. It was God that placed that picture in our hands so we would know while traveling down the road of uncertainty that there is certainty and purpose.

To this day, my sister and I speak of the photograph and give thanks to the stranger who took it. I am convinced, now more than ever, that God assigned an angel of photography that day because he knew its value went well beyond monetary measures. He in his ultimate wisdom knew that this stranger's photograph would warm two hearts and keep their spirits alive.

I know there is light in every dark room and God's love to warm every spirit. The secret is, however, to be brave enough to open the door once it's closed, so his grace may fill your heart with hope and purpose. It is for this purpose that I pray you see the light in your hours of uncertainty, and it is with certainty I can assure you it is there.

EXERCISE: *Positive Snap Shot*

What's really important in life? Sitting on a beach? Watching television or realizing the journey we are taking is worthy and deserves our all? Today, think about what it is that you appreciate in your life and the snapshots worth saving.

*Place a
Picture Here*

Tell about the Picture Here

"Some fisherwomen give more than just pearls. They give hope. If you're fortunate, the fisherwomen in your life will do just that."
—Lorna (Parsons) Stremcha

A PIECE OF ME

A Pearl of Hope in our Oyster Stew

Fishing the Madison, Missouri, and Gallatin; hunting for arrowheads; picking asparagus, dandelions, and mushrooms were common occurrences while living with Aunt Mae and Uncle Marvin. Along with spending time in the great outdoors came Saturday chores, something that really didn't bother me. After all, I had learned to tend for my brothers and sister at a very young age, so doing laundry and house cleaning with someone else was kind of nice. However, there was something I really didn't care for, and that was dinner.

Every Saturday night we ate oyster stew. It was a ritual. Uncle Marvin loved it, and Aunt Mae aimed to please him. I gratefully choked it down without complaint. Aunt Mae had inkling that the four of us didn't like it. I think it was probably more than inkling; it was probably written all over our faces as we sat and slowly put our spoons to our mouths. We ate very slowly—very, very slowly.

Aunt May was clever, and she figured out a way to help us somewhat enjoy our Saturday night dinners. Just before dinner was served, she'd sneak into her room and return. During dinner, she would talk about how oysters made pearls and perhaps one of us would be lucky enough to get one in our stew. It never failed. Every Saturday night one of us would end up with a pearl.

Now, I cannot be certain as to why she really did this, but I can tell you what I got out of it. Our life was in shambles. Our hearts were breaking. While Aunt Mae never showed her affection through hugs and kisses, she did show us that there is hope in everything. She and Uncle Marvin taught us rivers can be dangerous yet can give us fish to eat. Fields can be green, moist and messy; but if you look closely, they have many hidden treats to eat. Dandelions can be turned to wine. Arrowheads have many hidden secrets and tales. No matter how tough life gets, there's always a pearl of hope. Fortunately, I was able to speak at my aunt Mae's funeral and share my gratitude of these fond memories.

EXERCISE: *Get Creative*

How will you practice the ways of the fisherwoman? Below you will see some writing prompts. Refer to the poem if needed. If you do not want to write, paint a picture, or create a collage that represents the fisherwoman inside of you waiting to get out. Get physical and go fishing. Take a friend. Listen to the universe, pray for guidance, or simply meditate as you fish.

EXERCISE: *Writing Prompts*

I am a fisherman/woman because I _____

I have the patience of _____ because I _____

God loves fishermen/women because they _____

> "Knocking on the door doesn't always get you what you want, but sometimes it gives you what you need."
> —Lorna (Parsons) Stremcha

A PIECE OF ME

Mrs. Cornfield

Fear is an emotion that holds us back. It does not matter whether you are trying to lose weight, change careers, leave your spouse, break up with your boyfriend, start a new school, go away to college, or introduce yourself to a neighbor. Fear does not discriminate; it does not care how old you are, what color you are, what sex you are, or what religion you are. We all face fear at one time or another. As a child who grew up in and out of foster care with abuse and alcoholism, fear was an emotion I had to learn to manage.

In the fifth grade, I had the distinct pleasure of meeting Mrs. Cornfield. We were living in the country outside of Twin Bridges, Montana, and Mrs. Cornfield lived across the road. Mrs. Cornfield was an elderly lady caring for her terminally ill husband. Eager to get to know our neighbors, my brothers, my sister, and I walked across the dirt road on a Saturday afternoon, took a few deep breaths, and knocked on her door. Within a few short minutes, a small, fragile woman with a smile and a twinkle in her eye opened the door and invited us into her country home.

The four of us introduced ourselves, and she asked if we would like some cookies and Kool-Aid. Of course, we said yes. Then she took a book from the table, held it up, and asked if we would like her to read from the Bible. We all nodded yes. She then asked us if we would like to study the Bible with her on Saturdays. We said, "Yes!" She then explained tithing.

During the week, each of us would try to earn pennies, nickels, and dimes for Saturday Bible school. Every Saturday afternoon after lunch, we walked across the country road, knocked on her door, and were greeted with a smile. Mrs. Cornfield would arrange us in a circle, and we would listen as she read Scripture. She'd lift her collection plate, pass to the person on the right, and we would put our collection of coins in her dish. It didn't matter whether it was one penny or a hundred. Each penny mattered. And, most importantly, we knew we mattered. Every Saturday after our Bible lessons, she would feed us cookies and Kool-Aid.

As Mrs. Cornfield helped us manage our fears of abandonment, abuse, and alcoholism, we helped her manage her greatest fear: losing her husband to cancer. As we prayed in the circle together and lifted our Kool-Aid glasses in thanks, we all found strength from God every Saturday afternoon. To this day, the four of us speak of Mrs. Cornfield and her loving kindness and the lessons she taught us. The world certainly could use more Mrs. Cornfields. Helen Steiner Rice wrote: "What more can we ask our Savior than to know we are never alone-That his mercy and love are unfailing and he makes all our problems his own" (*Hope Springs Eternal*, 1978).

So what does this have to do with fear? It is simple: realize that you are never alone even when you must flee from your home in the middle of the night. If you search, if you ask, there will be someone in your life who will help you find the courage to conquer your greatest fears. Perhaps her name will be Mrs. Cornfield.

EXERCISE: *Open A Door*

Alexander Graham Bell once said, "When one door closes another opens; but we so often look so long at the closed door, that we do not see the ones which open for us."

Today, really look hard. Do some deep soul searching. Utilize the great mind you've been given. Think about the doors that have been slammed shut. Walk away, and don't look back. Open your eyes, really open them, and see the many doors waiting for you to step through. Choose one. Knock on the door and walk inside. Allow yourself to go places you want to go, meet people you long to meet, and take adventures you desire to take. Just knock. Knock on the door. Create these places, these people, and these adventures through imagination. Every goal, every dream begins in the mind.

Circle the letter or statement of your choice.

Which door will you see today?

A door of the past.
A door of the present.
A door of the future.

Which door will you open?

A door of the past.
A door of the present.
A door of the future.

Which door will you walk through?

> A door of the past.
> A door of the present.
> A door of the future.

What did you discover about yourself? Why?

"The experienced mountain climber is not intimidated by a mountain—he is inspired by it. The persistent winner is not discouraged by a problem–he is challenged by it. Mountains are created to be conquered; adversities are designed to be defeated; problems are sent to be solved. It is better to master one mountain than a thousand foothills."
—William Arthur Ward

A PIECE OF ME

Climbing the Wall

I am not, nor have I ever been, particularly fond of heights. So when I had the opportunity to climb the wall at the YMCA, I took the challenge. Guess what? I made it all the way to the top. I rang the bell and came on down. Today, I climb much higher mountains. I love it! My point is that sometimes the small triumphs to others are huge triumphs to us. So get moving, face your fear, and conquer it! What you'll more than likely find out is that it's not as frightening as you once thought.

EXERCISE: *Face Your Fear*

Today, I want you to confront things that are holding you back and take action toward conquering them. Here's what you're going to do: sit down, take a pen or pencil, and write three to five fears that are holding you back. After listing your fears, write some brief statements or phrases that will help you overcome such fears.

Fears:

I will overcome by:

"There are many ways to be free. One of them is to transcend reality by imagination, as I try to do."
—Anias Nin

A PIECE OF ME

The Power of Vision

When I was in high school, I was very involved in DECA (Distributing Education Clubs of America), a marketing club for high school and college students. I was scheduled to compete on the state level in public speaking. I had never competed solo in this area of speech before and found myself a little lost, confused, and somewhat afraid. However, because my teammates expected me to come home with a trophy, I soon expected the same of myself.

One of the first things I did was to find a person that I knew to be very successful in this area to coach me. Her coaching provided me with the necessary tools I needed to compete in extemporaneous speech, but the rest was up to me. Aware that my friend could not compete for me, I was forced to discover a pathway that would lead me to a successful destination. I began counting on my faith more and more; I opened my mind to the idea of visualization and incantations. After doing so, I relentlessly conditioned both my body and mind into nightly routines.

Every night for at least five minutes before falling asleep, I would visualize myself winning an award in this particular event. My focus became so clear that I could see the room I was competing in, the clothes I was wearing, the ice sculpture in the center of the banquet table, and me accepting my award. I did this along with self-talk for a month religiously.

Not to my surprise, everything went as planned. I came home with a top honor, which provided me an opportunity to go to nationals in Anaheim, California. So you see, believing is achieving. *How will you transcend reality by imagination today?*

EXERCISE: *Believing & Achieving*

- Think of something you would like to accomplish. Be realistic. Make sure your goal is something obtainable.
- Write the commitment down. Be specific.
- Find someone that can coach and lead you toward your goal.
- Take action. Ask for help.
- Set a schedule so you can develop your skills. Commit!
- Practice your skill.
- Picture yourself or the event as you want to be or it to be.
- Picture the details in color. Imagine the event two or three times throughout the day. Before you fall asleep, visualize the event in detail for five minutes. You must begin doing this well before the actual event. Defy reality!

DATA DUMP

Please forgive me for:

I forgive myself for:

P.I.E.S. Reminder

"A happy heart makes the face cheerful."

Proverbs 15:13 NIV

Chapter Three

Bullies, Abusers, & Weight Issues

Something to think about:

> "We define ourselves by the best that is in us, not the worst that has been done to us."
>
> —Edward Lewis

Date: _____
Today, I give thanks for

Signature: _____

"Sticks and stones break bones. Words fracture spirits and hearts."
—Lorna Stremcha

Bullies & Self-Image

Mean-spirited behavior and wicked words are like a cancer slowly eating away at your spirit. These things drag you down and hold you hostage.

Many of us unfortunately face a bully. I faced many in childhood and adulthood. Some of the meanest and most damaging bullies were those I encountered in the workplace. Sadly, bullying is wreaking havoc on our self-esteem, self-image, physical health, and mental health—regardless of age, race, religion, status, or sex. My research has revealed many others who are being bullied.

Bullies know how to destroy self-confidence. They also know how to create fear. When Mimi, a former teacher from Pennsylvania was bullied by members of her school administration, her self-confidence was one of the first things to go. Mimi began to question her every move, trying to avoid any action that would create more problems. She simply didn't know who she could trust, and was constantly on guard. She became angry. Mimi's anger grew from frustration.

As the mother of a special-needs child, Mimi found herself losing patience and self-control. She realized she needed to speak out and to find help. And she needed to continue speaking out until people began to listen. Only after Mimi felt someone understood, could she begin to regain control of her life.

Bullies can do a lot of damage to your self-image, and calling on reprogramming techniques can be a saving grace.

My experience with bullies in the workplace lasted almost a decade. I felt powerless, overwhelmed, isolated, ashamed, humiliated, and ugly. I felt like yesterday's trash! These were feelings I had never felt even as a child who had been abandoned and abused.

The point is, I get it!

I believe I can help you gain a better understanding about bullying and help you understand we sometimes bully ourselves and contribute to our own unhappiness and unhealthy habits. It is also my belief my experiences will help you gain a better understanding of negative self-talk and demonstrate the necessity of reprogramming.

Tim Fields, the author of *Bully in Sight: How to Predict, Resist, Challenge and Combat Workplace Bullying: Overcoming the Silence and Denial By Which Abuse Thrives*, defines workplace bullying as "the repeated mistreatment of one's employee targeted by one or more employees with a malicious mix of humiliation, intimidation, and sabotage of performance." Fields also refers to workplace bullying as psychological harassment and violence done to you by others. Zogby reported workplace bullying to be two to three times more prevalent than illegal discrimination, affecting one in six workers.

Bullies usually appear when someone in power or authority feels threatened by another person or subordinate that displays qualities and skills that they do not possess. *The bully's personality is dominated by his or her need to feel good.*

PSYCHOLOGICAL DAMAGES RELATED TO BULLYING

- Anxiety
- Depression
- Post-traumatic stress disorder (PTSD)
- Loss of confidence
- Low self-esteem
- Personality disorders
- Periods of unworthiness
- Permanent or semi-permanent feelings of hopelessness
- Panic attacks
- Periods of tearfulness and irritability
- Sadness
- Lack of concentration
- Forgetfulness

- Loss of humor
- Loss of joyfulness

Other forms of abuse also cause similar problems. Even after someone is removed from an abusive situation, the effects can be long-lasting. Another trauma or event can often cause these underlying problems to surface.

PSYCHOLOGICAL DAMAGE RELATED TO DOMESTIC VIOLENCE, RAPE, & CHILD ABUSE

- Experience PTSD
- Waking up in a state of panic
- Nightmares
- Flashbacks
- Obsessive behaviors
- Avoidance of pleasurable activities
- Isolating self from friends and others
- Sleep deprivation
- Inability to concentrate
- Lashes out at others easily
- Feels guilty
- Feels shameful
- Feels unworthiness
- Feels hopeless

PSYCHOLOGICAL DAMAGES RELATED TO WEIGHT ISSUES

Many people with weight issues have deeper problems. For this very reason, I suggest that you see a professional who can help you deal with your true emotions. If you fail to address these issues, you will keep repeating bad behavior. P.I.E.S is a vehicle to help you uncover your problem. It is up to you to take action and help yourself.

- Shame
- Guilt
- Isolation
- Unattractive
- Worthless
- Hopeless
- Low self-esteem
- Poor self-image
- Moody/emotional
- Flashbacks
- Lonely

SHARED PROBLEMS

Bullies: create health problems, social problems, self-esteem, and self-image problems.

Abusers: create health problems, social problems, self-esteem, and self-image problems.

People with weight issues: create health problems, social problems, self-esteem, and self-image problems.

EXERCISE: *Labels*

Write positive and negative labels given to you by yourself and others.

Your mother:

Your father:

Your siblings:

Your spouse or significant other:

Other family members:

Your friends:

Your teachers:

Your spiritual leader/minister:

Your employer:

Your coworkers:

Others:

Yourself:

Which messages played repeatedly in your head today?

Which messages are true?

List the negative messages:

List the positive messages:

List messages you feel you need to work on:

Dump the negative messages.

DATA DUMP

Please forgive me for:

I forgive myself for:

P.I.E.S. Reminder

"Remember no-one can make you feel inferior without your consent."

— Eleanor Roosevelt

Chapter Four

Overcoming the Bully Within

Something to think about:

> "Sometimes I try to convince myself that what someone else thinks is valid when it doesn't match my own ideals and sometimes it just seems easier to accept an idea or opinion that I don't believe."
> —Gracie Campbell

Date: _____
Today, I give thanks for

Signature: _____

We Bully Ourselves

We often bully ourselves. Do not try to tell me you do not do this. Ask yourself these questions. How many times a day do you complain about your hair, thighs, wrinkles, cellulite, nose, etc.? How many times have you said to yourself, "I'm stupid. I'm ugly. I'm fat."

You get the point.

As a weight counselor, I found that many of my clients bullied themselves so much that they didn't need help from actual bullies to lower their self-image.

Many of my clients convinced themselves they were bad or not good enough. With this kind of negative self-talk, it is difficult to like yourself and achieve success. If you tell yourself you are a failure, chances are you will create that destiny. If you tell yourself you cannot lose weight, you will not lose the weight. If you tell yourself you are going to fail the test, you are likely to fail.

You become your own worst enemy. By allowing such negative talk to control the true you, negative action is set in motion. Whether intentional or not, your thoughts become forms of action. You sabotage yourself.

I also believe that putting yourself down lowers your standards. By ignoring your strengths, you are slapping your God, your spiritual guide, in the face. Furthermore, you are slapping yourself in the face and those who have come to love you. By allowing negativity to control your beliefs, you are negating any positive feelings that others may feel for you. *Now, that's not very nice, is it?*

Stop allowing others to bully you. And stop bullying yourself. How do I stop my inner bully? (This is a lesson you will see repeatedly. It is that important.)

EXERCISE: *Self-Talk Revisited with a Twist*

Step 1: Look yourself in the eye and reclaim your awesomeness.

Step 2: Get present. Being present is essential while doing self-talk and creating change. Keep the self-talk in present tense ("I am ... " "It is ... " etc.). This keeps you in the moment.

Now repeat to yourself ten or more times a day while looking yourself in the mirror:

>I am worthy.
>I am wonderful.
>I am witty.
>I am bright.
>I am beautiful.
>I am talented.
>I am ...
>
>*Say whatever you have to; just stop the bully inside!*

EXERCISE: *The Twist*

Objective: To demonstrate negative and positive thoughts, words, and labels that enter our lives daily.

Needs:

- Active participant (You)
- Three–six large clear containers, jars, vases, or pitchers (You will need six if you work outside the house.)
- Pebbles, stones, marbles, buttons, paper clips, or coins.

Find three to six clear containers, jars, vases, or pitchers. Decorate them. You are going to want to make the jars, vases, or pitchers attractive as they are going to be placed in a visible location. They will be a tangible representation of your thoughts, feelings, words, and actions. Container number one is your spirit; your soul filled with all the positive and negative thoughts, feelings, words, or actions. Container number two represents the positive you. Container number three represents the negative you. For the next two weeks, these jars will be tangible reminders of the words thoughts, labels, and actions that you cast upon yourself, that others have cast upon you, and that you have allowed others to cast upon you or you cast upon others.

Place the jars, vases, or pitchers next to each other. (If you spend a lot of time at work, you will need six containers—three for work and three for home.) Label them "All of Me," "Positive Me," and "Negative Me." Find or purchase small stones or pebbles, marbles, beads, buttons, paper clips, or coins. It really doesn't matter.

Fill the container labeled "All of Me" with the stones, pebbles, or beads. Every time you speak or think a negative thought, take a stone from "All of Me" and put it in "Negative Me." Every time you say something positive, take one stone out of the "Negative Me" and deposit it in the "Positive Me."

Keep checking those jars. If you have too many stones in "Negative Me," keep working at it.

Finding Strength

> "I know that without prayer, without faith, and without asking for help in a spiritual way that negative, evil, and ill-spoken words can darken and rob the soul if these feelings are not combated with positive reinforcements."
>
> —Lorna (Parsons) Stremcha

Earlier, I alluded to bullies in my workplace, but I did not go into detail. I went down a path of darkness paved with post-traumatic stress syndrome and deep depression. This was something I had never experienced. This experience, while horrific, forced me to face many truths that had lain dormant for many years.

This four-year battle reminded me that in darkness there is light, and out of belief in one's self comes empowerment, commitment, courage, and strength. It also reminded me of the heroine, Anne Frank, and the introduction in the novel, *Anne Frank: The Diary of a Young Girl*, written by Eleanor Roosevelt. These particular statements made a profound impression.

> "Living in constant fear and isolation, imprisoned not only by the terrible outward circumstances of war but inwardly by themselves, made me intimately and shockingly aware of war's greatest evil the degradation of the human spirit. Despite the horror and the humiliation of their daily lives, these people never gave up. Anne herself and most of all, it is her portrait which emerges so vividly and so appealingly from this matured very rapidly in these two years, the crucial years from thirteen to fifteen in which change is so swift and so difficult for every young girl."

The courage and strength of Anne Frank and others who faced persecution should remind us that out of evil comes good and out of darkness there soon will come light. Do not surrender your power. Turn it into empowerment. Find the Anne Frank in you, and have the courage to combat that which tries to draw you into darkness and break your spirit.

While I use Anne and her story as an analogy, I admit that while my torment was not as vile and evil as that of the Holocaust, it was a battle. It nearly cost me life—something I hold precious.

While I was tormented by a mob of bullies, I didn't help the situation by beating up on myself. I implore you to stop bullying yourself. Surround yourself with people who lift you up and help you face truths in positive and supportive ways. Get help from professionals if you need to. Do not be ashamed. End the denial today.

Look at yourself in the mirror, and use positive self-talk daily. You are worthy and unique; you only get one chance at this wonderful thing we call life. Face your enemies, your bullies, your battles, the weasels, and the wars. Stop whining. Don't allow outside forces and internal battles to clip your wings or to break your spirit. Fight back, and reclaim yourself. Face yourself. Get real. Get honest. Get moving. Take action. Tell yourself how wonderful you are.

Positive self-talk is essential to help you create a healthier and happier you. Take it one step at a time. Stop the internal beatings and allow the bruises to heal. Positive self-talk is not the complete answer, but it is a start. Choosing healthy self-talk provides you with more strength to face your nemesis. It offers you the opportunity to enhance your emotional intelligence and look at the situation with more clarity. You are not allowing vicious words to bring you down.

For all practical purposes, self-talk should be simple, to the point, practical, and honest. Positive self-talk is essential; it provides a clear picture of what it is you desire. It opens the door of possibility. Realizing you are reading this book tells me that you want to be better. Speak only in the positive. Below you will find examples of negative and positive self-talk to help you better understand how to put your thoughts in the positive and present tense. Following these lists, you will find self-talk statements, which can be utilized in building a better self-image.

Negative: I can't do math.
Positive: I am capable of learning math.

Negative: I can't remember names.
Positive: I am able to remember names.

Negative: It's going to be another bad Monday.
Positive: It's going to be a great Monday.

Negative: I'm so stupid!
Positive: I am intelligent.

Negative: I'm too shy.
Positive: I enjoy meeting new people.

Positive Image Building Statements

- I am special. I like who I am, and I feel good about myself.
- I am unique, and there is no one else like me. That's amazing!
- I am glad to be me.
- I am intelligent.
- My mind is capable of learning.

- My mind is clever, quick, and alert.
- I am interested in learning and doing new and different things.
- I am organized and in control of my life.
- I am kind, sincere, honest, and genuine.
- I am all of these things and more. All these things make up me.
- I like who I am, and I'm _____

EXERCISE: *More Positive I Ams*

Write ten positive self-image statements. After you have written your statements, say them aloud. Now, look yourself in the mirror, and talk to yourself. Of course, you'll feel silly. I am telling you it works. Perceptions are powerful. Believe. Record your "I am" statements if you want. Play the recording repeatedly if you want. Hey, if you're up to recording yourself on video and sending your image of self out to the universe, just do it! Be positive.

I am_____

I am_____

I am_____

I am_____

I am_____

I am_____

I am_____

I am_____

I am_____

I am_____

DATA DUMP

Please forgive me for:

I forgive myself for:

P.I.E.S. Reminder

"When I release my burdens to the night, like a balloon to the wind I am free to experience my true self."

—Unknown

Chapter Five

Gratitude, Attitude, & You

Something to think about:

"Every day and in every way, I'm getting stronger and stronger."
—Anthony Robbins

Date: _____
Today, I give thanks for

Signature: _____

A PIECE OF ME

Patty's Strength

My friend Patty was out jogging. A seventeen-year-old boy intentionally ran her over with his sports utility vehicle. His New Year's resolutions were to kill someone, to have sex with their corpse, and to taste human flesh.

Patty endured twenty-four days of hospitalization. She suffered six fractured vertebrae, four fractures in her pelvis, a collapsed lung, and brain damage. If this was not enough, she was forced to relive the incident in a criminal law suit and then a civil law suit. The seventeen-year-old was sentenced to fifty years in prison. Her civil suit failed.

From personal experience, I can tell you that dealing with the courts are stressful. It requires drawing on strengths you never knew you had. It demands that you pick yourself back up in order to see light in the darkest hours. It requires that you talk to yourself and visualize that you will prevail. It requires surrendering to God or a higher power. It takes mental toughness.

Most people will never have to experience something so horrific, but they will face demons of some kind. This is when we must call on strategies and techniques to overcome them. Patty's belief in herself, her motivation, and her determination to right a wrong gave her the positive energy that helped her run her marathon. It is Patty's traits and her fortitude that make her capable of fighting her battle. It is her attitude that keeps her spirit alive and keeps her smiling. Her emotional intelligence keeps her going. It is her ability to ask for and to accept help when needed. It's her ability to walk through tragedy and visualize her way out that keeps her going. She realizes she will never be the same person she was before the incident, but the important thing is she is trying to be better every day. Patty believes in herself and has conviction.

EXERCISE: *Release, Convict, Visualize, & Take Action*

Do you have Patty's inner strength? Yes or No

If so, how do you plan on maintaining it?

If not, why not?

Do you have conviction? Yes or No

If so, how do you show your conviction?

Today, release your burdens to a higher power. If you are in need of professional help, get it. Pick up the phone and make an appointment. If you are having a problem with a friend or colleague, confront the situation. Be polite and sincere. Say what you mean to say, but say it nicely. "Mary, I didn't appreciate it when you criticized me in front of the boss. Next time you have a problem with some of my work, please tell me in private. We can work it out."

If you have too many responsibilities at work or in your personal life, prioritize. Pare down your obligations. Decide what is most important, and drop the duties that bring you down. Do this only after you have completed your promise. Visualize yourself as the lion. Picture yourself with courage and strength. Find your inner Patty. You are much stronger than you realize. I honestly believe that. Now, take action.

"Life is now in session. Are you present?"

—B. Copeland

A PIECE OF ME

The Importance of Being Present

Being present is essential in creating change. Being present is best explained as not allowing outside forces to distract you. My children both played sports. Both are very competitive and enjoy the thrill of a win, but more importantly, they enjoyed their sport. The ability to stay focused while on the ice, basketball court, volleyball court, or softball field required being in the moment each and every second. They had to be completely focused on what was transpiring at the time, at that very moment. They didn't have time for outside distractions like fans and screaming coaches. They were focused on the game. They were present. This is what helps create winners.

Another example of being present involves communication. Again, I'll use my children because I think most of us can relate. After school, my children usually were hungry, full of energy, and bursting with conversation. Many times, while in the middle of these conversations, the phone would ring. When I picked up the phone, I lost focus. This distraction caused their voices to lower and the sparkle in the eye to dim. When this happened, my heart would break. After all, they were sharing their day with me and an outside force interfered. The momentum was lost.

Because this disturbed me, I worked diligently at getting the present back by apologizing, looking them in the eye, and providing them with the knowledge that what they had to say was important.

Most of the time, I told the caller that I would call back after I finished with my kids. This helped my children realize that they were important to me.

When talking to yourself you must be present. Be conscious of you. You are important. When looking at yourself in the mirror or meditating, be aware of this. This knowledge will help you focus and communicate better. Looking you in the eye and being present with yourself are essential if you are to believe in you and your abilities. This is also essential in helping you develop a healthier self-image.

Self-talk must always be directed to achieve your objectives in a healthy and beneficial way. This means you must always direct self-talk in a safe way. This is because the subconscious mind does not know right from wrong, and the point of doing this exercise is to help create a better you. What we tell ourselves about our problems will affect our actions, and what others say or do to us can be even more damaging if we allow ourselves to believe them.

EXERCISE: *Practice Being Present*

Today, when your children, your friend, or your family member tries to tell you something, really listen. Remove all distractions, look them in the eye, and let them know they are the most important person in your life at that moment. Let them know you are really hearing them. Really listen.

Tips for better listening:

- Get a positive attitude
- Concentrate
- Pay attention to tone of voice
- Pay attention to facial expressions

- Pay attention to gestures and body language
- Avoid poor listening habits
- Daydreaming
- Pretend listening
- Don't interrupt
- Don't give up when the material or information seems difficult

"There is more hunger for love and appreciation in this world than for bread."
—Mother Teresa

Gratitude is to be thankful. Grace is to demonstrate thanks. An attitude in gratitude is essential if you are to honor your commitments and complete your goals. Gratitude and grace are essential if you are to become a self-advocate, develop a healthy self-esteem, self-image, self-confidence, and fill the empty void. For these reasons, we must learn to be thankful for our minutes and hours of grief, pain, sorrow, and sadness as well as our minutes and hours of happiness. For it is in these trying times, we are shown our true strengths and provided the opportunity to see the strengths and grace in others and ourselves. I give you a few stories of grace.

A PIECE OF ME

Grace in Paula's Final Moments

Paula was a fellow teacher. With her family and four close girlfriends by her side, she heard the diagnosis of a rare form of breast cancer and bone cancer. She went through years of chemotherapy, radiation, and surgery; she continued teaching until she was forced to resign. Teaching gave her a sense of inner peace and focus.

When it became evident that her days on this earth were ending, I crawled deep within myself to understand our purpose as friends. This is what I walked away with after hours of inner dialogue. This is also part of the letter I gave to her family.

"Never take a day for granted. Appreciate life, appreciate a few extra pounds, appreciate each breath and living thing. Go outside while you can, because someday you may only be allowed twenty minutes. Walk every day because someday you might not be able to walk to your own kitchen without help. Embrace the warmth of the sun and the colors of the earth; take in their beauty. Treat people with compassion; be brave; be kind; say "thank you," and if you can't do it yourself, ask for help because good friends will help. Love completely and with an open heart. Enjoy the dance because it ends quickly. Find peace; make it if you have to. Love your God; thank him for each breath, each day, each and every thing and person who comes into your life. If that thing or person brings you pain, embrace it and thank him anyway."

EXERCISE: *Go Beyond Self*

Volunteer; go beyond self. Visit a friend, and let them know how very important they are to you. Gather with your friends, and create something. This can be a painting, a stained-glass piece, a scrapbook, a poem, or a quilt like the one we did for my friend. This way your important person is always covered in grace.

Just take action!

"Grandmothers help us make sense out of our past. It is up to us to take control of the present. It is within our power to create our visions of the future and see that the job gets done."
—Lorna (Parsons) Stremcha

A PIECE OF ME

Grandma Parsons

To look at her and listen to her, you'd never know she was sixty-seven years old. We baked a cake for her, brought her presents, and made her queen for a day. That was Sherrie Marie's idea. Grandma beamed as she wore her crown.

Grandma Parsons was a stable force in my life, a person who taught me much about gratitude and humility. She was a mentor and a simple woman with immense wisdom. What I admired most about Grandma Parsons was that no matter how awful her life, she always greeted it with appreciation and a smile.

Years later, Minnie (Wilamina Adams) Parsons' spirit resulted in a *Bozeman Chronicle* feature in the column "A Day in the Life of Bozeman." The story titled "A Montana Life" ran on April 8, 1997, and depicted a grandma I very much loved.

The story began with her passing a beach ball across the room. She was ninety years old at the time. In the article, she shared her stories of riding bucking broncos, camping and fishing in the backcountry, attending school in town, and ranching in the Gallatin Gateway.

She spoke of her diabetes and how it affected her eyesight. She shared her desire to earn a nursing degree and how over the years she delivered sixty-five babies.

Grandma died February 21, 1998. She was a woman who always saw the good, no matter what her children and grandchildren did or were doing. Grandma Parsons was not a complainer. She was a fighter and a survivor. She was a constant in my life. She gave me strength.

She and Grandpa gave me the gift of thanks and appreciation for nature in all its glory. They are why I stop and pick litter off the ground and give thanks for the good given to me. Thanks to them, I find the mountains, the rivers, and the oceans a place of serenity and grace.

I will forever be thankful for the many nights she combed my hair, the tales she told me of her youth, the times I rubbed her legs when they were in pain, the patience and love she showed four little grandchildren after their mommy ran off with the carnies, and the help she gave my daddy giving me a Thumbelina Christmas.

Grandma Parsons gave me abundant gifts of love, compassion, optimism, and kindness effortlessly; and because she did that, I am able to do the same. These gifts have given me the strength to survive my own tests. Sometimes I thought that my grandmother was looking through rose-colored glasses and denying the truth, but who am I to judge?

Grandma Parsons was a woman of mercy (without a nursing degree) who helped bring hope into the world by opening the door of possibility to every person she knew. She looked after me. She was a nurse and a teacher with an abundance of love to give. While others may describe her differently, I can offer my truth and the lessons she taught me.

Along with such lessons came the art of conversation and storytelling while snapping beans at the kitchen table. Because she insisted that I shouldn't cry when she detangled my hair, I learned to cope and to grin and bear it. If she hadn't taken the time with me when I was very young, I would have lost the ability to see good in most things. Most importantly, I might have missed the lessons she taught me each time I visited—always believe in a higher power and keep dreaming, even in the darkest of hours.

When I think of Grandma Parsons, I hear the lines that we often shared.

"What's ya wanna be, Lorna Mae, when you grow up?" she'd ask, and I would reply, "I wanna be a big star, Grandma!"

Then she'd assure me, "You can be whatever you want to be. You know, your grandpa was in a few silent movies."

I can't say that I'll ever understand how she could honestly be proud of what some of her family had become. Maybe she simply chose to see only the good and to avoid the pain by denying the evil. No matter, she loved her family of wrongdoers, and for that I'm grateful.

Whenever I entered a room, her eyes would light up, and I knew that in my grandma's eyes I was a star. Even after glaucoma and blindness set in, each grandchild, no matter their indiscretions, knew that they were a star who helped light Grandma's world. To know true love is the greatest gift, and that's my gift from Grandma Parsons. I just hope that when my own children enter a room they can see by looking at me they're my lights and my stars.

EXERCISE: *Queen for a Day*

Make someone queen for a day. Take the time, and make a crown. Use cardboard, old jewels, use recyclable materials, use whatever you want. Create a special day for the queen in your life. Pamper her. Record her special days; put it on a disc; watch it with her; give it to her. If you prefer, create a few scrapbook pages for her and gift the day to her. Make her feel special. In turn, you will feel as if you were given the world. You will be rewarded with grace.

"We must cultivate our garden."

—Voltaire

A PIECE OF ME

Nana's Lessons

Alice (Billman) Cobb was my mother's mother. I called her Nanny or Nana. She was committed to her family, friends, community, and country. She introduced to me volunteerism, politics, Walter Cronkite, and Lawrence Welk. She encouraged my love of reading and nurtured me when I needed it. Nanny was a stabling factor in my life. Her teachings demonstrated what P.I.E.S. represents and graciously taught me many life lessons. Lessons given are worthy of sharing, so with a warm heart I share my nana's lessons with you.

Nana's Life Lessons

RESPECT YOUR COUNTRY

Red corn poppies, candy canes, Royal Neighbors of America, and political propaganda covered the dining room table and floor at Nana's house on B Street in Livingston, Montana. At her insistence, I handed out red corn poppies to a passerby on Veteran's Day; from her voice, I listened to the words of "In Flanders Field" by Lieutenant Colonel

Tammy McCrae. And because the red poppies invaded my play area, her dining room, I listened intently to the words.

In Flanders Fields

In Flanders Fields the poppies blow
Between the crosses row on row,
That mark our place; and in the sky
The larks, still bravely singing, fly
Scarce heard amid the guns below.

We are the Dead. Short days ago
We lived, felt dawn, saw sunset glow,
Loved and were loved, and now we lie
In Flanders fields.

Take up our quarrel with the foe:
To you from failing hands we throw
The torch; be yours to hold it high.
If ye break faith with us who die
We shall not sleep, though poppies grow

BELIEVE IN YOUR GOD

Just as she taught me the importance of honoring the veterans by handing out red poppies, she showed me the significance of the candy cane, which affirms the foundation of God's promise.

The Candy Cane Legend

Look at the Candy Cane
What do you see?
Stripes that are shed for me
White is for my Savior
Who sinless and pure!
"J" is for Jesus my Lord, that's for sure!
Turn it around
And a staff you will see
Jesus my shepherd
Was born for Me!

As with everything Nanny did, it had a deeper meaning, so it shouldn't come as any surprise that the insurance she chose to sell came with a mission.

CHOOSE WORK WITH A PURPOSE

In 1968, she was appointed district deputy for Royal Neighbors of America, selling insurance for a fraternal life insurance society for men, women, and children from birth until age sixty-five. Royal Neighbors was important to Nanny. If she dropped by unexpectedly, it usually was to invite us to the annual Royal Neighbors of America banquet. Amazingly, everyone in the family honored her request and showed up. Prepared for snapshots, we dressed in our Sunday school clothes because with Nanny and Royal Neighbors came a shopping bag of film for photos. Most of us hated our pictures taken, but we smiled and obliged because it made her happy. Because Royal Neighbors of America was important to her, I was inducted into the society in a formal ceremony during my senior year in high school.

ALWAYS BE WELL GROOMED

Nana had a sense of style. She always dressed well. Her nails were manicured; her hair was styled; her shoes were shined; her makeup always looked fresh. She bought me my first pair of black patent shoes and my first Elizabeth Arden makeup kit.

DANCE

Her love for socializing was something else that can't be denied. She loved to dance and attended parties and dances until Papa Joe passed away. Because I knew how much she loved to dance on occasion, I would join them at the senior center and dance with Papa Joe as Nanny stood in the background and smiled.

WATCH YOUR WEIGHT & EAT HEALTHY

Good role models practice what they preach. I would rise to the sound of Doris Day singing on the radio, a bowl of cream of wheat or oatmeal, half of a grapefruit, a piece of toast, and a cup of tea with one lump of sugar and a teaspoon of cream. Snacks were limited, especially sweets. Outdoor exercise was mandatory, and if we couldn't find something to do, she would come up with a chore that kept us busy.

KEEP LEARNING

Nanny was a smart woman. Smart women read. Nanny bought books for me. She even allowed me to lay under the covers and read *Old Yeller*, or my chosen novel, by flashlight. She encouraged my curiosity by allowing my older cousin, Don, to read to me from his high school text books while he babysat.

WATCH THE EVENING NEWS

The evening news with Walter Cronkite was taken seriously. We sat silently and watched together every night.

BE CHARITABLE

Charity is important. If you have no money or belongings, giving your time is just as important. Nanny demonstrated this daily. She volunteered for many service activities and often brought me with her.

FOLLOW THE GOLDEN RULE

Nanny never said much but was my role model. She always treated people as she expected to be treated. "Do unto others as you would have others do unto you."

Think about what your grandmother or grandmothers gave you. Remember it and pass it on. Do you make someone's eyes light up? If so, who?

EXERCISE: *Become a Mentor or Cook Chicken Soup*

List lessons given to you from a grandmother, mother, or mentor. Share your lessons with others. This may require volunteering, tutoring, lecturing, or simply sharing time with a family member, friend, or stranger in need. Make some homemade chicken soup or your favorite soup, and drop it off for a friend if you want. Here's my favorite recipe:

LORNA'S CHICKEN NOODLE SOUP

> 12 to 16 cups of water
> 4–6 skinned chicken breasts
> 1–3 bouillon cubes or you can used canned bouillon (according to taste)
> 2–4 stalks of celery (you can leave the leaves in if you want)
> 6–8 green scallion onions with stems (chop)
> 1 medium onion (chopped)
> 2–4 medium carrots (sliced)
> Add Mrs. Dash spices for soups or your favorite spices
> 3–4 cups of egg noodles (frozen or dried) (I add this after the chicken and veggies have simmered.)

Place all ingredients except egg noodles in a large pot, and bring to a boil. Reduce heat; cover; and simmer for 2–3 hours until chicken is tender. Add more water if necessary. Cut chicken after cooked into bite-sized pieces. Return meat to pot, and add noodles. Continue to cook for about 25 minutes. Make sure the noodles have absorbed the flavors. Serve. Enjoy!

"Adversity brings knowledge and knowledge wisdom."
—Proverb

A PIECE OF ME

Skills I Learned from the Miss America Program

Commitment is essential when trying to obtain any goal. I was fortunate enough to compete in the Miss Montana/Miss America Pageant. Though I did not win the state title, I did come away with life skills that I have been paying forward ever since. Understanding the program's value, I was able to utilize many of my acquired skills while managing and counseling at top weight-loss clinics and centers. The centers and clinics I worked for extended this knowledge with schooling and practical experiences.

Good fortune allowed me to attend conferences put on by *Glamour* magazine; attend workshops with Dr. Covert Bailey, author of *Fit-or-Fat*; attend Diet Center's Nutrition and Behavioral Modification School; and participate in continuing education courses and workshops by Dr. Wayne Dyer, author and visionary. The knowledge I gained from these experiences has taught me much about commitment.

Preparing for Miss Montana/Miss America requires huge commitment from its contestants. It also demands a great deal of personal responsibility, sincere humility, knowledge, loyalty, and sincerity. The program also teaches that there is always room for improvement, along with the essential need for preparation and hard work. These are some skills I was able to pass on to a group of juvenile girls in Portland, Oregon.

One of my clients was having difficulty reaching these girls. The more we talked, the more we learned about one another. After sharing some of my childhood and teenage experiences with her, she became convinced that I was the one that could reach these girls. Her goal was to persuade them to attend school and graduate. I realized that the girls thought she didn't understand their situation. She had no clue where they were coming from. She asked me to meet with them, and I agreed.

In just a few short minutes, we bonded. We connected. They knew I wasn't going to fill them with a bunch of BS and listened intently as I talked to them with a completely open heart. The intense conversations that followed my speech prompted tears and sighs of relief. Someone understood! They knew truth! Realizing the girls trusted me, I challenged them to each make a commitment. This commitment required that they attend school and graduate. It demanded that each of them give their best because they needed this for their futures, for their future children's futures. After persuading the girls to sign the contracts, I placed the contracts in a folder and handed them to the client who arranged the meeting. Because follow-up is vital, we continued to meet until I moved back to Montana. The next year, I received a beautiful card announcing that all but one of the eleven girls graduated from high school; some were attending vocational schools while others chose college.

The point is that these girls had to make a personal commitment in order achieve their goals. They worked through their adversities in order to meet their goals. Just as Miss Montana/Miss America and life experiences have taught the power of commitment and follow-through, it also reinforced gratitude. The importance of gratitude should never be understated. I recall coming to this conclusion as a young child.

> "There is no such thing as gratitude unexpressed. If it is unexpressed, it is plain, old-fashioned ingratitude."
> —Robert Brault

A PIECE OF ME

Remembering Gracious People & Moments

As director of public relations, I had the opportunity to train many amazing girls and work with some of the most caring and generous people in the country. The director of the state pageant impressed upon us all the value of a thank you. The pageant constantly reminded girls, "Do remember all sponsoring organizations and all the wonderful people that helped you attain this goal." Most of the girls thanked their sponsors and mentors graciously. I am privileged to remain in touch with many of the girls. Each time I see or hear from one of them, "thank you" is always attached. Now, that is a great dose of gratitude. For this, I am grateful.

Another encounter of grace and gratitude occurred when I entered the campus of Rocky Mountain College. I had nothing except makeup, clothes, some bedding, and less than $300 in my checking account. I had no home and no place to call home. I had graduated from high school and was released from my foster home. My life was my responsibility. I was confused and frightened, yet determined.

Chaplin Robert Holmes, college minister and professor, and Professor James Taylor, Ph.D., the director of financial aid, came to be my cheerleaders, my rocks, my counselors, my spiritual guides, and my warriors. They took me under their wings and taught me how to fly. They encouraged me to try new things, taught me to face monsters, and demanded that I seek help, something I wasn't very good at doing. Their kindness and grace are memories I will forever cherish. Precious is the time they freely gave.

Some of my fondest memories of Chaplin Holmes are kept in a flowered folder on the third shelf of an armoire in our family room. Among other words of wisdom is a crumbled and faded piece of paper with the paraphrased Shakespeare quote, "All the world is a stage and we are all fundamentally actors." The actual quote comes from *As You Like It*, Act 2, Scene 7, which reads as follows: "All the world's a stage, And all the men and women merely players; They have their exits and their entrances. And one man in his time plays many parts, His acts being seven ages."

Thirty years ago, Chaplin Holmes gave me that note. It's reminiscent of many kind people and helps me to appreciate them more. Their faces and voices are ingrained in my memory and offer hope when I face dark moments, moving me to smile when I think of them. They help me hold true to the idea that life is simply to be created; life's dramas are to be perceived as acts. New scenes sometimes require new cast members; all acts come to an end, and with curtain call come goodbyes. So appreciate the scene for what it is, for there are more scenes to follow and more lessons to be learned, and always give thanks to the actors that give you a piece of their hearts.

The gratitude for these men and the kindness of Rocky Mountain College will forever be a gift that I hope to reciprocate someday. To teach a person the value of self and the courage to face the truth is a generous gift, which continues to help me as I walk through this life. It is also a gift that has taught me how to regroup and continue to find hope in the darkest hours and the courage to start over.

EXERCISE: *Collect Quotes*

Go through some of your favorite books, or search the web for your favorite quotes. Find an old picture that makes you smile. Copy the picture, cut it out, and paste here. Put a suitable quote underneath. Go one step further. Attach your favorite quote to a homemade gift, and give it to someone special.

> "Gratitude is one of least articulate of the emotions especially when it is deep."
> —Felix Frankfurter

Give thanks; write a letter to God, Buddha, an angel, a friend, a family member, or to yourself. Just get in the habit of doing this more often than not. You don't need to do it every day, just often enough so you can be reminded of the positives in your life. It is crucial to date and sign your letter because it will allow you to see how much you are developing and changing in various aspects of your life. In this letter, express your gratitude, and then simply ask. You may wish to ask for strength, courage, love, peace, wisdom, guidance, etc. Make sure your letter is written with respect and sincerity. Make sure it is legible; after all, it is for someone very important. Read your letter over, kiss it, smile, and tuck it away. Okay, you do not have to kiss it, literally, but do find a nice place to keep these letters. I suggest placing the letters in a nice journal or a box.

How to Write a Thank-You or Social Note

A friendly thank-you note does not require you to share stories and information. Instead, you share a very short social message. The message may be a thank you for a gift or someone's kindness. Because we are talking about gratitude, we are focusing on the thank-you note. You can write your note with special paper, make a special card, or buy a special card with your thank you inside. A thank-you note is usually one or two paragraphs in length. The paragraphs are short, to the point, and include the same components as the gratitude letter.

KEY COMPONENTS

1. Heading: address and date (address is only necessary if you are sending your letter to someone). The heading is located in the upper right-hand corner of the letter.
2. Salutation: Dear ...
3. Body: the message
4. Closing: Your friend,
5. Signature: Your name

Here's an example:

> Dear Grandma,
>
> The book and game you sent me are wonderful. I am on page 137 and cannot wait to find out what Mary does next. We have been playing a game of Scrabble every Wednesday night after dinner. The game has helped with my spelling skills. Last week, I earned a perfect score. I surprised myself.
>
> You always seem to pick the perfect presents. I especially enjoy reading the notes you write to me. They make me feel important. I just wanted you to know how much I appreciate your gifts and words.
>
> Love,
> Lily

Journaling

Journals provide opportunities for us to practice our writing, to experiment, to activate thought, to stretch our minds, to tackle problems, to reflect, to express ideas, and to collect thoughts. Journals can be kept in a notebook, on a computer, or in blank books made especially for journaling.

I started practicing gratitude and forgiveness journals years ago during the time my mother was in the care of a hospice. I found the experience to be profound, so I decided to pass the lesson down to my students. Today, many of them continue to practice journaling memories, gratitude, or forgiveness for special and important people in their lives. It is a very intimate way of expressing self. Journals allow you to express feelings you may have a difficult time expressing aloud. The journal itself can become a keepsake for the family. It is quite a profound gift.

A PIECE OF ME

Forgiveness & Gratitude Letters

Death is profound. It is difficult. It is sad. It is emotional. How we handle the passing of a family member or a friend is important. There are no right ways. There are no wrong ways. However, having experienced many losses due to death, I am certain there are healthy ways. As you have to come to realize, my mother had her flaws, as we all do. Her mother abandoned her. Her brother died at an early age, and she never got over it. She was abused by many men and unfortunately at times abused others. She drank too much at times and gambled when she shouldn't have. Sadly, she denied herself the opportunity to know that a woman should be loved and treated with respect.

    I knew my mother's heart. It was a good heart. She didn't always make good decisions. Who does? We all make poor choices. Some of us are just more equipped or have better resources to help us. She needed help. She never got it. Because she believed and felt she had no support, she suffered the majority of her life. No matter, she did the best she could, and she created a huge footprint on my heart as she did those that truly knew her. She kept me when she could have aborted me. She held my hand when I gave birth. She fought battles with the courts to win us back. She did the best she knew.

    Her last few days on earth, she read the journal the family left for her. We wanted her to know she was forgiven. She needed to know we held no hatred toward her. More importantly, we wanted her to know her life served a purpose, and she needed to forgive herself. Her children, her grandchildren, daughter-in-law, nieces, nephews, and many close friends wrote in her gratitude/forgiveness journal. Before Mom died, I placed her journal on her coffee table. I wrapped it in purple tissue paper. She opened the journal a few days before she surrendered her life to God and the angels. This is one way we dealt with dying.

After Mom's death, I continued to journal. It helped me grieve. However, I truly believe what helped most was that I listened. I listened to that little voice inside of me. The voice that nagged, "She needs to know she is forgiven. Forgiven by those that matter most, her children. More importantly, she needs to forgive herself. You need to help her with that." Perhaps you have a voice nagging at you. Perhaps you need to be forgiven or provide someone in your life with the knowledge you forgive them. So today write your letters of forgiveness and letters of gratitude with care and kindness.

Steps in Creating a Gratitude/Forgiveness Journal

- Purchase a nice journal with lines. Many people will be writing in this journal, and having lines makes it much easier. If you cannot afford or find a journal to purchase, a composition notebook will do. They can be found where school supplies are sold.
- Pay attention to the cover. The cover of the journal should reflect the person's personality, special hobby, special quote, or poem. For example, when Mother was in the care of a hospice, I purchased a Wire-o Journal. It is purple with a painting of a vineyard on the cover. If you are creative, design your own cover.

- Appoint a caretaker for the journal. This is important because this person is responsible for getting the journal to all the people that desire to write in the journal. They also are responsible for retrieving the journal, wrapping the journal, and delivering it. I suggest a sign-off sheet with a deadline date. This makes it easier to pass the journal.
- Be respectful, and be nice.
- Include the date for every entry.
- It must be handwritten. Write neatly, legibly, and use a dictionary.
- Write from the heart. The memory you share must be thoughtful and kind.
- Sign your entry.
- Pass the journal to the next person.

EXERCISE: *Demonstrate Your Gratitude*

Write a letter of gratitude to a higher power, write a thank-you note to someone special, or begin a gratitude journal for someone special. If you really want to be creative, send a message in a bottle and set it free in the river or ocean, or send a special note out to your favorite social network. If you like the dirt, plant a garden or tree in memory of your special person. Sign up to walk in a marathon, bike-a-thon, or fundraising event like Relay for Life or Walk for the Cure. Take action, and demonstrate your gratitude.

DATA DUMP

Please forgive me for:

I forgive myself for:

P.I.E.S. Reminder

"Before you close your eyes, pause and give thanks for the amazing people in your life."
—Unknown

Chapter SIX

Commitment, Promises, & Pledges

Something to Think About:

"Any resolution or decision you make is simply a promise to yourself, which isn't worth a tinker's damn unless you have formed the habit of making it and keeping it. And you won't form the habit of making it and keeping it unless right at the start you link it with a definite purpose that can be accomplished by keeping it."
— Albert Gray

Date: _____
Today, I give thanks for

Signature: _____

About Commitment

As young girls, we may join a club or an organization and make a pledge or promise. As a former Girl Scout and an executive for Treasure State Girl Scouts of America, I lived by the Girl Scout promise and law. I still do today. Some habits are worth keeping.

I am committed to many promises. I am committed to my marriage and my two children. I am committed to making this world a little better place by getting involved in organizations like CASA, causes against domestic violence, feeding the hungry, donating blood, being an organ donor, standing up against bullies and abusers, and participating in mentoring groups.

As a certified educator, I am committed to helping those who wish to learn. As a coach, I am committed to training the competitor to be his or her best. As a facilitator, I am committed to helping others develop positive life skills and habits as well as positive work skills. As an individual, I am committed to waking up every morning and trying to be the best me I possibly can be that given day.

Commitment is not easy. It is time-consuming. It is not perfection. It is following through. It is getting the job done, completing the assignment, following the weight-loss plan, the exercise plan, the Girl Scout Promise, the Educator's Code, completing the task. It sometimes feels like you are swimming upstream like the salmon. It is sometimes feels like you are breaking through walls. It is climbing mountains. It can be difficult. It can be done. Commitment is essential to success. Fortunately, I am a half-glass-full gal and now can offer you some insight. A fair warning, you will not always like what you hear or what is asked of you. For this very reason, you need to commit to change. However, before you begin, it is only fair that we examine what it means to commit.

As we make and keep commitments, even small commitments, we begin to establish an inner integrity that gives us the awareness of self-control and the courage and strength to accept more of the responsibility for our own lives. By making and keeping promises to ourselves and others, little by little, our honor becomes greater than our moods.

—Stephen Covey

What is commitment?

- The act of committing
- The state of being committed
- A pledge or promise
- An obligation

SYNONYMS:

- An obligation
- A pledge
- A responsibility
- An engagement
- An assurance
- A duty
- A promise

COMMITMENT TAKES:

- Time
- Effort
- Courage
- Dedication
- Desire

- Flexibility
- Fortitude
- Stick-to-it-ness
- Willfulness
- Belief in one's self
- Belief in one's abilities

Thomas J. Watson, Jr., author of *Business and Its Beliefs*, writes:

> ... the basic philosophy, spirit, and drive of an organization have far more to do with its relative achievements than do technological or economic resources, organizational structure, innovation, and timing. All these things weigh heavily in success. But they are, I think, transcended by how strongly the people in the organization believe in its basic precepts and how faithfully they carry them out.

Simply put, commitment is difficult and time-consuming. This is why most people fail to meet their promises and resolutions. Commitment requires us to change. It requires us to develop new habits and to take the time to develop new habits. Commitment can cause us discomfort. Change is not comfortable. Change can be frightening.

Commitment Means Dumping the Negatives

Committing sometimes requires dumping old habits, old friends, moving, or changing directions. Change your old habits. Get rid of the negative influences. This will light a fire. Commitment means taking action.

P.I.E.S. requires action. It requires you to commit to change and to grow or develop in the areas of physicality, intellectuality, emotionality, and spirituality. Simply put, if you are truly bothered by something, you will want to change it. Get honest with yourself and list the negative habits, people, and things in your life. Do not sugarcoat or try to rationalize. Surround yourself with people you most want to be like. If you want to lose weight, join a gym. If you want to get a better job, take some classes. Just stop making excuses.

EXERCISE: *Dump the Negative*

- List the negative habits in your life.
- List the negative people in your life.
- List the most common reasons you fail to get the job done.

Check the excuses that best help you rationalize.

- I don't have the time.
- I'm too tired.
- I can't afford it.
- I don't know anybody at that event.
- I have never done that before.
- I failed the last time I tried that.
- I don't like to _____

Commitment means faithfulness to self and others. Promises are meant be kept. For many individuals, these promises are very sacred and are literally taken to their grave. However, for some they are easily broken.

It is important when you make commitments, such as a wedding vow, you truly are committed to making the marriage work. That you are going to give your best to follow through with your contractual agreement. Granted, some contracts fail. This begs the question *why*.

Why did I fail to complete my contract, my obligation, my promise? Did you fail because you knew in your heart that it was the wrong thing to do? Did you fail to realize that the commitment required would take a lot of work?

It is likely that you failed to meet your promise of obligation because you did not realize that true commitment takes persistence with purpose. Perhaps you truly did not believe in the goal. Maybe it was just the thing to do at the time, or you felt pressured by outside forces or other people.

I believe that with consistency and purpose most things are achievable. I believe that you are your best investment. The reasoning behind this is simple. If you don't believe in yourself, who will? If you are not going to work to achieve your goal, your commitment, how will you achieve it? It is up to you.

Teachers in Montana are asked to commit to the Code of Ethics for Montana Educators. As leaders, we make a commitment to helping others achieve their dreams, their goals, and their desires. Effective leaders do this by committing to the premise of continual self-improvement. They share the spotlight and credit others that helped them become effective leaders. They possess personal integrity and self-control.

Positive commitment coupled with values, ethics, and principles provide foundations, which helps to maintain commitment. This, in turn, provides success and promise. When you put your actions into motion with integrity, purpose, concrete goals, and objectives, it is easier to stay committed.

Commitment is challenging. It sometimes requires that you listen to constructive criticism and respect others and yourself. Commitment according to P.I.E.S. means that you dedicate yourself to you in your efforts to change. It means that you give the best of you on the given day as you take your journey. It does not mean perfection; it simply means committing to being your best each and every day. I get that commitment is difficult. That is why the journey takes dedication, diligence, and time.

Commitment takes practice. It takes you getting up every day and fulfilling your promise. If your promise is to improve yourself in the areas of physicality, intellectuality, emotionality, and spirituality, then you must intend to fulfill the obligations each and every day. If you want to lose weight, you need to follow your eating and exercise plan each and every day even after you have lost the weight. If you want to improve intellectually, you need to commit to learning something new each and every day. If you want emotional balance, you must learn to control your emotions each day. If you want to improve your spirituality, you need to open your heart, pray, forgive, and give thanks to a higher power each and every day. Commitment is seeing that the job gets done. Commitment is dedicating yourself fully to your team. It is not quitting when the going gets tough. It is being fully convicted no matter how difficult. Some commitments are marathons; some are sprints.

Commitment Means Setting Goals

EXERCISE: *Goal Setting*

It is not enough to simply picture your goals. You must put the pen to paper and set your goals. Magical things happen when you write goals out and read them in black and white.

Let's begin.

- Collect your tools.
- Get focused.
- Write your name and date on the paper.
- Write four ultimate goals.
- Reread what you just wrote.
- Get specific.

How do I write my goals?

Let's use a weight-loss goal to illustrate the process. Pretend you weigh 153 pounds and are a female of medium stature. You desire to be at your ideal weight, which is around 118 pounds. Now, let's be real. You haven't weighed 118 pounds since your wedding day. Dig deep, and figure out what exactly it is that you want.

Do you want to be healthy and happy, or do you want to be miserable trying to achieve something you really don't want? I am guessing you want to be healthy and happy. We've established that 118 pounds for you right now is unrealistic and isn't going to happen. Now, determine your ideal weight.

The first step in setting any goal is to realize what it is that you wish to accomplish and then confronting yourself with reality. Let's begin this process logically. What can I live with?

You establish 130 pounds to that livable number. You even applied logic. You came to this conclusion because you weighed 130 pounds for the majority of your married life. It was only a few springs ago that you started packing on the weight. Recently you got a glimpse of your behind in a mirror. Ouch! Doughnuts and pizza have taken over the rear. Wow, major reality check! You then strip yourself naked and find the courage to confront your reflection. Who is that person? Oh, it's me. It's been a very long time since you've really looked at yourself honestly. You are appalled and utterly disgusted with yourself. You are so upset you decide to lose weight.

You don't know what to do. You pout a little, maybe even cry a little, beat yourself up, and complain a lot. You get mad at your significant other because he failed to mention the fact that you were carrying a wide load. You lash out at your kids because they insist on Toll House Chocolate Chip cookies, and you chew your best friend out for not saying anything. Okay, enough is enough! It's time to take action! That's exactly what we're about to do.

Let's get started; grab a pen, tablet, journal, or just a plain piece of paper and start .

Getting Started

Write as follows: I, _____ weigh _____ and desire to weigh _____. I will accomplish this by: _____

- admitting that I need help
- making an appointment with someone that will hold me accountable
- ridding the kitchen of unhealthy foods
- donating unopened foods to a food bank
- buying foods on the LPS grocery list found at the end of the book
- realizing that perfection is not the goal
- realizing that losing weight takes time, patience, and hard work
- drinking my six to eight glasses of water
- eating on schedule and eating only foods on the program
- practicing better eating habits
- regarding meal times as opportunities for conversation and socialization
- eating to fuel my body to maintain a healthy lifestyle
- establishing an exercise routine
- utilizing relaxation and positive oral self-talk exercises
- consciously making an effort to do a random act of kindness
- avoiding negative situations and negative people
- celebrating my accomplishments at the end of the day
- treating myself with positives like reading, watching a movie, getting my nails done, etc.
- practicing breathing exercises three times a day.

You get the point. However, because this goal will take a lot of time and hard work, you need to break it down into baby steps so you can have some immediate gratifications.

> "If you don't like something, change it. If you can't change it, change your attitude."
>
> —Maya Angelou

A Piece of Me

Preparation, Diligence, Realities, & Accountability

Preparation and diligence are keys to achieving anything. As an educator, my class motto was, "Diligence is the key; the more you put into it, the more you'll get out of it." By following the motto, my students came to realize they would be working hard. Some of them whined, and some relished it. But they all knew their efforts would be rewarded.

An example of this involved two of my eighth-grade students. During lunchtime, the principal came to me with two homework packet assignments that were due after lunch. The students had been given one week to complete the homework. The boys chose not to use wise management skills and found themselves with incomplete work. So, like many adolescents, they contrived a plan. Unfortunately for them, the principal caught them. They admitted to stealing someone's packet and copying it. Whether they admitted to the cheating or not, they were still busted. The great thing about the admission is that it showed that both boys possessed a conscience. After meeting with the boys, the principal brought the homework packets to me and explained what had happened.

The packets remained on my desk until the end of fifth period. After the fifth-period bell rang, I asked the boys to stay after class. I shut the door and explained to them that we needed to discuss their packets after school. After school, both boys entered my classroom. I asked them if they had cheated. Both answered yes without excuses. *Good*, I thought, *at least they are honest*. I then told them they needed to call their parents and explain what had occurred. Each boy called his mother. After the confession, I got on the line. I told their mothers I was going to make up a new packet for them and have them come in after school for a few nights until the packet was completed. The mothers approved my plan.

The easy thing would have been to give the boys a zero, but this would not have taught them personal accountability, responsibility, or ability. The boys also had to rake leaves and clean windows at home. Not only did the boys learn a lesson in honesty and integrity, they learned the value of the assignment and what it had to offer them. They learned to be prepared, utilize time more wisely, and that hard work does have benefits.

Aspiring to do anything beyond mediocrity takes hard work and preparation. Desiring to reach for something that seems unreachable takes due diligence, a good attitude, conviction, and time. It takes sweat, tears, and a strong constitution, as well as the ability to take disappointment and rejection. Being prepared makes it easier to pick you back up and start over.

However, for preparation to be fully appreciated, it is vital that some truths be confronted. These truths may not be easy to digest but nonetheless must be confronted. Failure is one thing, but setting yourself up to fail is another. So in your preparations for your future successes, your goals must be attainable.

If you have set a goal to become a medical doctor, then you had better have an aptitude for science and math. And you had better be able to achieve good grades and be willing to give up some fun.

If you want to be a professional singer, you had better have the raw talent that can make this possible. You also need thick skin because you are more than likely going to be criticized and rejected. You also must be willing to devote time to practice and get some coaching. After all, there is always room for improvement, and there will always be someone that you can learn from.

If you want to lose one hundred pounds, you have to admit you need to quit eating fattening foods, bad carbohydrates, and find someone to help you get moving and eat right. You better have the courage to get on the scale in front of someone else, and in the privacy of your own home get naked and really take a really good look at yourself. You had better be able to toss away the junk food, sodas, and extra garbage that is keeping you fat. You must be willing to admit that you are the one responsible for your weight problems, and be ready to take action toward helping yourself. After all, you more than likely wouldn't be in this predicament if you had your life together.

If you want to be a scholar, then you need to be prepared to dedicate your life to books and academia. Whatever your goal, preparation is key, and along with this comes personal responsibility.

Taking responsibility is an obligation. You owe this to yourself and to those who believe in and love you. So be your best! Create the best you. It's simple: have the courage to admit what you perceive as failures and weakness and work on fixing them. Take inventory, and find out what you do best and make it better. Focus on the positives in your life. If you are a good mother, be a better one. If you are a good teacher, become better. Keep in mind being better does not mean giving up joy or fun, nor does it mean being perfect. Being better simply means challenging yourself to another level and continually setting the bar higher. It means taking responsibility and being accountable for you. It means making yourself a symbol of idealism.

Paying attention to your appearance, your manners, your intellect, your creativity, your abilities, your talents, and your spiritual needs will enable you to show the world the truly gracious person you are. It also helps to admit that there is always room for improvement, and taking action is the only way to get this done. So don't just dream it; create it.

Whatever your dream, knowledge is key. With this understanding, the concept of achievement becomes a reality. That is why one must continue to feed the mind with new ideas and knowledge.

"Everything big starts little."

—Brian Tracy

Mini Goals

Mini goals are easily obtainable because they are done within short periods of time and should not create stress. They allow us to stay focused and driven because we can see some colors of the rainbow at the end of each day.

Here's how to establish your mini goals. Ask yourself what it is that you need to accomplish today to ensure that you have a successful day. This can be one thing, or as many as ten, as long as they are realistic and easily obtainable. Prioritize so you don't get upset with yourself if you don't complete everything on your list. These goals do not have to be related to your weight in any way. They can be simple tasks that gnaw at you just because they need to be tended to. After you accomplish one goal on the list, cross it out and move to the next.

Don't let events stop you from reaching your mini goals. If you get a call or email asking you to do something, make a note. If necessary, add that requested action to your list. Don't let outside influences distract you. Keep working on your mini goals. By the end of the day, you'll more than likely notice some things weren't completed. Don't worry; remember you prioritized, so study the list, and marvel at your accomplishments. Remember, you have tomorrow. Just simply move those that you didn't get to, to the top of the to-do list or goal sheet. Now, reward yourself with something pleasant that does not involve food, such as a facial, a bath, a movie, or quiet time. Just take time out for you.

See, you're feeling better already! Even though you have accomplished some mini goals, I must stress that you must never lose sight of your ultimate goal. Actually, I suggest you write your goal weight daily, and busy yourself by focusing on the mini goals. Before you know it, you'll have achieved your ideal weight for you and be ready to stabilize and move on with another big goal in your life. Remember, always be real, be honest, and celebrate your accomplishments. *Don't let others stand in your way.*

> "We are judged by what we finish, not by what we start."
> —Anonymous

Saboteurs seem to creep out of the woodwork like goblins and ghosts on Halloween night. Their presence is more prevalent, especially when we are trying to accomplish something important. They can't help themselves. It's their nature. You need to be prepared. Some people enjoy watching others fail. Seeing you change is frightening for those who love and care about you. I have found that it is especially difficult for family members. Be prepared to battle the saboteur. This is war! Like Joan of Arc, you need to lead the battle.

Sadly, and more often than not, you are your own saboteur. So be on guard. The more you know, the better equipped you are to fight. Before we go any further, I would like you to answer some questions regarding your inner saboteur. Honesty is essential!

EXERCISE: *Self-Inventory*

Do you like yourself? Circle Yes or No

Do you sabotage yourself? Circle Yes or No

If yes, please explain how.

What do you like about yourself?

What don't you like about yourself?

Why do you want to lose weight?

Why do you want to change?

You probably listed many negative things about yourself. Here is some information about Lori and Shannon. Read about them, and compare yourself to these two women. Lori is an eighteen-year-old college student. Shannon is a nurse and mother in her forties. Lori has gained the freshman fifteen pounds. When reflecting her feelings, she recorded she felt unintelligent and embarrassed. Shannon, the forty-year-old nurse with over forty pounds to lose, wrote that she disliked herself and felt her outward appearance was unsexy.

When asked why they wanted to lose weight, both women specifically stressed to prove they could do it and to show others and themselves. They also expressed that losing their weight would provide them with better health, more self-esteem, and a better self-image. These similarities are vital to acknowledge because both women appear to rely on the idea that losing the weight is what will make them happy and healthy. Granted, the weight loss helps, but it is not the key to developing a healthier or better self-esteem and self-image. It certainly isn't the key to self-happiness. Egos are fragile; when we constantly degrade ourselves and hear others say how stupid, foolish, ugly, fat, unattractive, and crazy we are, we begin to believe it.

Simply put, if you don't like yourself and are telling yourself that you are unintelligent, foolish, unattractive, and unsexy, you will believe it. Not only did these two women reflect that they felt this way about themselves, but they both expressed that they believed others perceived them as unattractive, unintelligent, and unworthy. However, they have no idea how others really see them. The actual problem is the perception of self.

If you constantly say negative things to yourself, you will believe it. So the questions are: Do these two women need to see themselves differently? Do you need to see yourself differently? How can you begin to change your negative thoughts into positive thoughts? How can you change what you refuse to acknowledge? To help you understand, I have decided to share with you a pledge I made to myself in 1977. Remember that college girl? I confess that that girl was me. I had put on some weight and wanted to take it off. I was feeling down about myself for a multitude of reasons.

A Piece of Me

Freshman 15, the Pledge, & My Promises

I had graduated from high school and no longer felt comfortable living with my guardians, so I moved out. The experience, though only for a few months, was very stressful. Every penny I made was going toward rent and college. Life was tough.

In late August, I loaded up my car, which didn't take long. I had nothing but the essentials: clothes, makeup, and a few dollars, which needed to go toward school. I had mixed feelings. One minute, I felt excited; the next, confused; the next, embarrassed. However, there was one thing—I was determined.

I pulled up to Widenhouse Hall at Rocky Mountain College and unloaded. I organized my room, which didn't take long. Having nothing to do, I wandered the halls and introduced myself to the girls on my floor. Life had changed. It was a bit frightening, but nothing like I had experienced as a kid. I felt fortunate. I was safe, had a place to sleep, and had three meals a day. My new life had begun. It was my chance, my opportunity to really make a change. It was my chance to make a difference and to put my past behind me.

My past had never been an excuse, so I was determined to turn my life into something meaningful and to become someone who could make a difference. However, insecurities set in upon entering my first accounting class.

I didn't have an affinity for accounting, but it was required as a prerequisite course. Like many freshmen, I had dropped some of my disciplines, which included exercise and mindful eating. No matter, college life progressed as normally as it can be for a college student. The truth is, nothing is normal when you're a college student.

College life is traumatic for some people, while those conditioned to trauma and dysfunction generally remained unfazed. However, some news can set off even the most complacent.

As the year progressed, a young man on campus started pursuing me while I was still dating my high-school boyfriend. My high-school boyfriend was attending school in Oregon, and I was attending Rocky Mountain College. We decided it would be okay to date other people. I had feelings for both young men, which put me in the middle of a relationship triangle. My emotions were a mess.

Thanksgiving weekend, my high-school boyfriend visited me at college, and our nearly two-year relationship ended. We were both blessed with the realization that we were too young to commit, so we made the decision to break up and went our separate ways.

As if mixed up emotions weren't enough, my mother, with whom I had not spoken for months, began calling me after the bars closed. My mother was difficult to deal with while under the influence. Her calls were stressful and depressing. Along with problems of the heart and guilt from my mother, I was taking a college peer counseling class and suppressed memories started coming back. Life was confusing. I began spiraling into a deep depression. I felt alone, overwhelmed, and confused. I began believing I was in this alone, but in reality, people cared about me and loved me. I just couldn't see it.

I was emotionally ignorant! Everything was foreign! Nothing was the same! In some regards, this was good, but it still was unfamiliar and frightening. Mindless eating and lack of exercise created another problem. It was December. The snow was falling and the outdoors was calling, so I took out my favorite 501 blue jeans. They were snug. I squeezed my chubby butt into them, but they were tight. Yuck! Mortified, I decided to do something about it. Disgusted by my appearance and unable to purchase a new pair of 501s, I decided to commit to change. This would be nothing new. Change, that is. I was flexible. I had to be. My life had always required I be. So instead of taking a walk, I wrote a pledge of commitment to myself.

Promises:

- I will start my exercise routine today.
- I will follow it faithfully every day.
- I will drink eight or more glasses of water daily.
- I will not listen to anyone who tells me that I do not have to improve.
- I refuse to be a fool and degrade myself.
- I will be the best possible me I can be.
- Each day I will make sure my hair is shampooed, my nails are clean and manicured, and my skin is clean, soft, and clear.
- I will strive each day to improve myself.
- I will not dwell on being overweight; instead, I will do something about it.
- I will become the best I can be for those who I love and who have faith in me.
- I will become better each day.
- I will prove to others that I can be much more than what they realize.
- After I lose my weight, I will continue to follow my habits.
- I will feel better about myself.
- I will prove to others that I have faith in myself.

- I will prove to others that I am what I believe I can be.
- I will begin being the person I want to be starting now.
- I will not make excuses to eat fattening foods. I will just say, "No, thank you," and walk away.
- I will take this one day at a time.
- I begin now ...

Nearly thirty years later, a friend handed me a book that included some of her personal commitment rules regarding weight loss. The similarities are uncanny.

Shannon's Personal Commitment:

- Increase self-esteem.
- Fit into my clothes.
- Get a better outward appearance.
- Feel sexier.
- Improve health.
- Prove to myself, "I can do it!"
- To show others, "I can do it."
- To live a longer life.

As you can see, we were both striving to fill voids.

EXERCISE: *Write your own promises or commitments*

Stay in present tense and begin each sentence with I will or I am. The first two are done for you.

I will ...

I am ...

DATA DUMP

Please forgive me for:

I forgive myself for:

P.I.E.S. Reminder

"Change is not a threat to your life but an invitation to live."
—Angel Wisdom

Chapter Seven

Change

Something to Think About:

> "Ever tried. Ever failed. No matter. Try again. Fail again. Fail Better."
>
> —Samuel Beckett

Date: _____
Today, I give thanks for

Signature: _____

Understanding the emotions that accompany college life, I decided to write my daughter a letter. I am sharing it with you with hope that it personalizes the kinds of conflicts that girls face when they leave home.

A Piece of Me

A Letter to My Daughter

There are just some things a mother needs to retell her beautiful, talented, and intelligent daughter. And because you know me so well, I'm sure you expected nothing less. So here it goes. You will embark on one of the most influential, empowering, exciting, challenging, and vulnerable times of your life. I want you to welcome these times; all of them, but especially the challenging and vulnerable times. For these times will teach you the most about your authentic self. "What the heck is she talking about?" That's probably the question you are asking yourself right now. Don't worry; you'll get the answers soon enough.

You are blessed with a brilliant mind, a loving and caring heart, and a compassionate soul coupled with a beautiful face and body. A piece of advice: don't take these blessings for granted. Care for them with respect. Be grateful for all your blessings; thank God and the universe for them. Use your gifts to help others. Use your gifts to help yourself so that you can help others.

This means always do your best. And when your best doesn't seem to be good enough or doesn't feel like your best, realize that you can do better. Try! Try! Try! When you feel like you've failed and fallen flat on your face, get back up right away. The sooner you get up, the easier it is. If you need help getting back up, ask for it. Know your family and true friends are there to pick you up and carry you if you need it. You can handle anything as long as you remember to surrender the burdens to God. He will sustain you. He does sustain you.

College life can be confusing. You're somewhat on your own. With that comes choices—you get to go to bed when you want, go to class, skip class, or partake in questionable activities. You are somewhat on your own. Life hands you choices. And so far, you have made very smart ones. However, scientific data and college presidents all share a common knowledge: between the ages of eighteen and twenty-five, many young adults often make very foolish choices. These choices can cost you, so, a piece of advice: make smart ones.

Choose to get enough sleep because if you don't, you won't want to get up and go to class in the morning. This could cost you a dream. Maybe, just maybe, this will be the day the professor reviews notes for the upcoming exam. Eat healthy because if you don't, you'll gain weight and struggle to lose it the rest of your life. Exercise daily, even if it's only for a half hour. It helps get rid of the negativism. Study hard; the payoff will be worth it.

Get involved in campus activities; you might find out something new about yourself. Meet new people. Try new things. Enjoy college. Don't be afraid to change your mind. You always have the excuses that you're young and a college student, or you can use, "It's my prerogative; I'm a woman."

Be true to yourself. Be selfish! Make college about you, you, and you! Don't feel guilty about it. This is one of the only times in your life you will get this opportunity.

Love,
Mom

P.S. Some last thoughts:

- Know your parents love you.
- Know we are very proud of you.
- Know you can tell us anything.
- Be true to yourself.
- Don't drink or do drugs.
- Always keep your dorm doors locked.
- Be careful in parking lots and on highways. There are a lot of weirdos out there.
- Don't wash reds with whites.
- Be good to your roommate.
- Don't get caught up in drama.
- Keep your room clean.
- Eat healthy.
- Exercise your body.
- Challenge your mind.
- Pray; be thankful and forgiving.
- Make college about you, you, and you!
- Have fun!

That was a difficult letter to write. I still choke up when I read it. I do not like having my children away from home, but things change. Change is difficult. The bottom line is that we all need to support each other, and we need to take care of our daughters and friends. We need to help ourselves. If that means writing promises, putting personal commitments on paper, or writing a meaningful letter with pieces of advice, then do that. If you need professional support, get it. If you need a gym buddy, then get one. You'll be helping your friend too. If you need more help, then get it. Whatever you do, be kind to you.

EXERCISE: *Get moving. Eat healthy. Be positive!*

Put on your walking or running shoes, and take a walk. Start tracking your steps. You should walk at least thirty minutes a day and strive to take 10,000 to 15,000 steps a day. If you are feeling sad because you have to say good-bye to someone special, write a letter. If you have a picture or pictures with you and that special someone, frame it, wrap it, and put the letter with it. Be creative, and get that body and mind moving.

> "It is our attitude toward life that will determine life's attitude toward us."
>
> —Anonymous

Attitude, Action, & Change

- Good attitudes beget good results.
- Fair attitudes beget fair results.
- Bad attitudes beget bad results.
- Sometimes we need to simply seize the moment. We need to stop, lean on a shoulder, and just embrace the moment so we may change a negative thought or negative feeling or a physical pain.

A Piece of Me

Reaching for the Sky

I was sitting on the curb with Goober who was crying from the excruciating pain in her leg. She leaned against my shoulder as I tried to console her. As we sat, she cried for her mom. She ached; she wanted her mom, but her mom was with my mom, and they had been drinking all night. So we sat together on the curb watching our siblings ride their bicycles against the gentle summer wind. We watched as they freed their hands from the handlebars and reached toward the sky. They were carefree. Their smiles were infectious. Goober tried to smile. I smiled. Their energy was contagious. It was powerful. For one moment, Goober had forgotten the pain from the tumor in her leg and smiled. This unspoken energy moved all of us to forget the negative pains we were feeling shortly before the bicyclers reached toward the sky with joy.

We pass unspoken thoughts and feelings to others. Let this simple act of child play lead you toward that positive energy. Stand under the big blue sky or the big gray sky, and reach toward it and smile. I just bet you will make someone else smile too. If that doesn't happen, realize the joy simply reaching up gave you. If you are daring, ride your bike and raise your hands from the handlebars, looking up and reaching toward the sky as the wind blows in your smiling face. If you feel less adventurous, just keep your hands on the handlebars, look up for a second, and smile.

EXERCISE: *Really Look at the World*

Today, I want you to go outside. First, go out for an early morning walk. Notice the dew on the grass, and feel the coolness from the night. Notice the quiet, free from traffic and noise. Hear the birds singing and the sprinklers going as they water the lawns. When you arrive home, get yourself a warm cup of coffee or tea. Sit outside; enjoy the quiet, the solitude. Close your eyes for just a few minutes; then open them. Notice how much greener the grass is, how much more vibrant the flowers are. Notice how much clearer you hear the sounds of nature. Look around you. Feel the warmth of the sun on your face. Embrace the moment. In the evening venture outside. Look up and see the vast universe and the stars in the sky. Smell nature and all its fragrances. Smile, lift your arms up high, and say a quiet prayer of thanks.

"The world hates change, yet it is the only thing that has brought progress."

—Charles Kettering

A Piece of Me

Coloring Your World

We have the power to control our lives. We do it every day. We are just not always aware of it. I'm not saying we have the power to control life, but the power to create our world. Granted, bad things happen. It's what we take from those experiences that are important. It is our attitude that breaks us, that can clip our wings. Each of us has the power to control our attitudes. We have the power to look at our world as full of color or as beige. I went through a beige stage. I even purchased beige furniture. I really do not like beige, so this surprised many of the people that have known me for years. It even surprised me. Beige is neutral and safe, but I have always been a person that likes purple, pink, yellow, and green. Truth is, I am not a beige person nor have I ever been.

To me the color beige has come to symbolize stress, pain, and sadness. My attitude resulted from the fact that shortly after purchasing this very dull beige furniture, my life was whisked into a world of chaos and distress, filled with miserable hardships. My attitude toward this color was negative and brought me down. I allowed this color to darken my heart, put me in states of sadness, and remind me of a horrific people and times.

Living in a beige environment stifled me. It made me feel insignificant and empty. I felt faded and dull. Unable to take me as beige, I decided to purchase paint. To ensure that I followed through, I spoke with a good friend that works in the home-decorating business. She suggested I take a brush and slap the paint on the wall. "I guarantee it will empower you," she said.

Taking her advice, I slapped a deep red paint on the biggest wall in my living room. Low and behold, she was right. Just taking action sparked the courage and energy I desperately needed to get through the mountains of lies that had been made up about me. It changed my attitude. It also helped my attitude toward beige.

I possessed the power to change the color and more importantly my attitude toward it. Just as I had the power to change my attitude toward beige, you have the power to create the change you desire. It is this simple; you need to alter your relationship with yourself. You need to learn to like yourself again. You need to find the person in you that brings smiles and happiness into your life. You need to change your attitude about you. You have the power to alter your attitude toward you. I am not saying that it is going to be easy. In fact, I did not say anything about this was easy. It is your attitude toward change that is key. Try using some of these techniques.

EXERCISE: *Attitude-Changing Techniques*

- Talk about something that reminds you of happy times.
- Surround yourself with only positive people.
- When confronted with a negative experience, see through the darkness; see the positive.
- Stand outside, and look around. Now close your eyes for two to five minutes and hear the whispers of the earth. Slowly open your eyes, and see the world's beautiful, vibrant colors.

- Stand in thanksgiving every day.
- Do something unexpected for someone important in your life. Better yet, do something nice for a stranger.
- Get moving: take a walk, a bike ride, a run, or garden. Get outside and fill your spirit with fun!

People that have a good attitude conduct themselves in certain ways. Life is beige only to beige people. Life is dark when we choose to see only darkness. Change your perception, your attitude. Next time you find yourself feeling dull or beige, color your world. Use my techniques. If those suggestions do not work, order yourself some beautiful, vibrant flowers. I do this. My florist just laughs.

> "It's easier to limit yourself, but if you do, you will never reach your full potential."
> —Unknown

To change is to make different. Change is to transform, to appear different, or to undergo alterations. Change is to move or go from one phase to another. Change requires altering an approach or attitude.

- To accept is the willingness to take or receive.
- Acceptance is the act or fact of taking something offered or given.
- Acceptance of change requires willingness to change your way of thinking so you may transform.

A Piece of Me

Changing Seasons

It was Indian summer; the school ground was covered in colors of fall. It was the beginning of a new school year. I was in the fourth grade, and we were living with foster parents. Change was inescapable. Flexibility was essential. Believing in a higher power was necessary.

Karen and Al were our foster parents. Their home was located on a hill that overlooked the school grounds. They were good people. They provided us with shelter and food. They also made sure we did our chores and practiced scripture. On weekends, we would visit the colony and attend the Mennonite church. We'd stay all day. I found it to be a very pleasurable experience. I did find it a bit strange, however, that Karen let us watch *Dark Shadows*. I can't say with certainty she actually let us watch *Dark Shadows* because she was probably too busy canning and baking.

Nonetheless, our fascination with *Dark Shadows* extended to the school grounds where we would build castles out of leaves and pretended to be cast members from the television show. We'd play that silly game until dark. Besides my interest in vampires, I had an affinity for Barbie and Troll dolls. Though we never owned any, we were fortunate to be friends with the three Stevens girls that lived across the street. They were a beautiful family, and I treasure their kindness toward Dairene and me.

A huge family with seven kids lived up the block. Both parents were deaf, and all the kids spoke sign language. They shared their language with us, and I got pretty good at it. The adversity and love in this family was so profound that I carried it all the way to the stage of Miss Montana as I danced, mimed, and signed to the Christian song "Giggle" by Amy Grant.

With changing seasons came changing locations, and during my fourth-grade year, we were once again uprooted and transported to Belgrade, Montana, to live with new foster parents. Flexibility comes with change, and it's just part of being a foster. You don't get too close, and you don't get too comfortable. You get used to change!

As we grow, we change. Our bodies change. Our noses might become bigger, our feet might become larger, we may develop strange bumps, and things just begin to change. So as time passed while living in Belgrade, Montana, with my aunt Mae and uncle Marvin, my body began to change. Not too quickly, but it began to change, and by the time I hit fifth grade, I needed a training bra because my breasts had started to bud. This disturbed me. One thing that bothered me even more was the fact that my feet were long and narrow. I was petite and scrawny, and my feet didn't fit my body.

Lucky for me, my cousin Marvin Junior was a newlywed. His wife, Lois, was fascinating. I thought she was the smartest woman alive except for the beautiful girl at the swimming pool who reminded me of Ali MacGraw. Though I never saw the movie *Love Story*, I did catch glimpses of Ali's beauty from Lois's magazines. Lois was a great conversationalist and very wise about female development and hygiene. So when I was feeling insecure about my changing body, she assured me that I would someday grow into my feet. Can't say as I really ever have liked my feet all that much, but I am glad to have grown into them.

It's amazing how life comes full circle and thirty years later you get an e-mail from a dear friend reminding you that you can start a wonderful new phase in your life. That change is an opportunity to do something challenging and positive that you've always wanted to do.

My hope for you is that you change with the seasons, be more flexible, and look at yourself in a new and positive way. And just as I have had to learn over and over again change is evitable, it is the way in which we receive it that makes its journey memorable and accepting.

"The indispensable first step to getting the things you want out of life is this: decide what you want."

—Ben Stein

A Piece of Me

The Hallmark® Card

I told Nanny everything. I really didn't want to tell, but I needed to for self-preservation and to achieve the life I wanted. Realizing I was going to say good-bye to my mother, I walked downtown to City Drug Store and searched for the perfect Hallmark card. It had to be perfect because I was telling her good-bye. I wrote my mother and told her how I just couldn't take her drinking and the strange men she brought home anymore. I told her I wanted more for myself. I told her I loved her and said good-bye.

    I left the card on the kitchen table and walked away with nothing but a change of clothes. I went into hiding for two weeks. Then I started a new life, in a new community. I understand most people don't have to make such huge decisions in order to accomplish a goal like graduating from high school or college; however, this life lesson helped me to understand the importance of planning and the power of taking action. The reality is that sometimes we must make difficult decisions and face disturbing truths in order to accomplish our goals and create change.

EXERCISE: *Take Action*

Stop hiding and take that first step toward a new you. Sit down and really think about what you want out of life. Think about what is holding you back. Don't be afraid. If you don't know how to get where you want to be, pick up the telephone, send out an e-mail, or knock on a door and ask for help. Create a plan, and take one step toward your new you. Take action! Enjoy the beginnings of a new you.

> "What lies ahead of you and what lies behind you is nothing compared to what lies within you."
> —Mohandas K. Gandhi

A Piece of Me

Mental Toughness

Achieving mental toughness is so difficult, there are actually people who make a living teaching it. Developing mental toughness takes effort, which every competitive person knows. Coaches are constantly telling their team members to be tough mentally and physically. As the wife of an ice-hockey coach, I have seen my husband express this to his team. As a mother of athletes, I have seen my children benefit from its discipline. As a former debate coach, I used it to help my team manipulate and outwit their opponents. As a former weight-loss counselor, I used it to help the client understand the necessity of finding that champion inside. As a teacher, I used it by requiring hard work and due diligence. As a mother, I used it every day by instituting rules of follow-through and stick-to-it-ness.

Mental toughness is a necessary ingredient that very few weight-loss counselors share with their clients. As a child growing up in a world of chaos, addiction, and abuse, I called on my mental toughness several times a day. Of course I had no idea what I was doing, but that is what it was.

As a plaintiff in state and federal lawsuits, I was forced to call on my mental toughness, my inner drive, and my positive self-talk repeatedly. It wasn't always easy, but it was crucial, just as it is for you to call on your mental toughness. Mental toughness is necessary in anything we wish to accomplish. It takes mental toughness to get the job done.

Some will argue that mental toughness is a personality trait, while others argue it is environmental. I argue that it is inside of each of us. We all have the internal desire to succeed. What many lack is the drive and willingness to work toward our success. Mental toughness is intrinsic. It comes from within. It is self-belief, positive self-talk, self-motivation, strong conviction, and integrity. It comes down to understanding and knowing yourself.

Dr. Smt. Jolly Ray, a level III hockey coach, defines mental toughness as the ability to consistently sustain one's ideal performance state during adversities in competition. Performing to one's potential requires good technique and mental skills. Ups and downs in performance are often directly traceable to psychological vicissitudes. Players who create a special atmosphere within them perform consistently. Mental toughness is learned, not inherited. The ultimate measure of mental toughness is consistency.

Ray's fundamental characteristics of mental toughness are:

- Self-confidence
- Self-motivation
- Negative energy control
- Attention control
- Visual/imagery control
- Attitude control

David Yukelson, Ph.D., Coordinator of Sports Psychology Services, offers the following definition.

"Mental toughness is having the natural developed psychological edge that enables you to generally cope better than your opponents with many demands (e.g., competition, training, lifestyle) that are placed on you as a performer. Specifically, to be more consistent and better than your opponents in remaining determined, focused, confident, resilient, and in control under pressure." (Jones et al, 2002).

Below you will find some key psychological characteristics associated with mentally tough, elite athletes (Jones et al, 2002).

SELF-BELIEF:

Having an unshakable belief in your ability to achieve competition goals.

Unique qualities that make you better than your opponents.

MOTIVATION:

Having an insatiable desire and internalized motivation to succeed (you really have to want it).

Ability to bounce back from performance setbacks with increased determination to succeed.

FOCUS:

Remain fully focused on the task at hand in the face of competition-specific distractions.

Able to switch your focus on and off as required.

Not being adversely affected by others performance or your own internal distractions (worry, negative mind chatter).

COMPOSURE/HANDLING PRESSURE:

Able to regain psychological control following unexpected events or distractions.

Thriving on the pressure of competition (embracing pressure, stepping into the moment).

Accept that anxiety is inevitable in competition and know you can cope.

No matter who defines it, mental toughness requires:

- Self-belief
- Self-confidence
- Motivation self-motivation
- Negative energy control
- Positive energy control
- Attention control
- Focus
- Composure/handing pressure
- Visual/imagery control
- Attitude control

You cannot allow self-doubt to undermine your confidence or focus. You may not be competing against anyone, but you are in competition against yourself. You are running marathons and fighting battles constantly, whether on a ball court, ball field, track, treadmill, fighting a legal battle, defending yourself against bullies, tending to children, giving birth, or trying to pass through the birth canal.

Life is a marathon. There are times we run a little slower, breathe a little deeper, struggle to climb the hill, stumble on our way down, mourn the loss of a family member, friend, or pet, but there are also times we rest on level ground in comfort. Life has its highs and lows. How we handle and perceive everyday occurrences is what is important. Why not get the edge by allowing yourself to use some of these skills used by thousands of people every day? You may not be a professional athlete or a high school varsity ball player, but you are in this life to be the best you can be. Use these techniques; strive to acquire these characteristics. Give yourself a chance. You are competing for your life!

Think about times when you maintained consistency, found solid ground, and called on that mental toughness. I'll bet you'll come to the realization that you were embracing the power of you and your belief in yourself. Believing in yourself is what has gotten you this far.

Find that competitive, positive person once again. Dig deep within yourself to find that self-confidence that you long for. Self-confidence can be practiced. You just have to believe in you.

Self-motivation can be taught. Just walk through the adversities. Stay focused. Keep your eye on the ultimate goal. Dump your negatives. Pay attention to your self-talk, take control of the way you perceive yourself and see yourself reaching your goal. Dig deep and play your life with consistency and strength. Become emotionally intelligent. Utilize self-talk and mental toughness to help you achieve your dreams.

"Everybody can do something that makes a difference."
—Todd Wagner

A Piece of Me

Tears of Courage

The McGuire Memorial Conference on Family Violence commemorated the homicide of Dr. Isabel McGuire and her two young daughters, Katherine and Jennifer. Dr. McGuire's abusive second husband killed all three and subsequently killed himself. These crimes deeply affected the Billings medical and professional community—my husband and I among them. Approximately five months after the tragedy, her former husband, Dr. Brian McGuire, and a number of community professionals organized the first conference. It took tremendous strength for him to share his story, to go on living, to continue contributing. I share his story, my family's stories, my friends' stories, and my stories of violence, of death, of illness, of loss, and of abandonment to demonstrate the need to dig deep within yourself to understand that you must change your attitude if you are going to move forward and not merely survive.

Deeply moved by Dr. McGuire's story, I approached him on a break after his speech. I told him how much his story had affected me.

He responded with tears in his eyes, and I paraphrase: "You know, Lorna, I have not been able to allow myself to have other children."

We sat briefly in silence. Then I left. Memories of the day I learned about Dr. McGuire's former wife and children flashed before me. I was sitting at the kitchen table with my cup of coffee reading the

Billings Gazette. My children were sleeping; the house was still and quiet. After reading the article, I sat numb in disbelief. Silence. Silence. Silence is what I remember. Tears welled up in my eyes just as they did the day I sat listening to Dr. Brian McGuire. I imagine, tears well in Dr. McGuire's eyes every day.

I tell McGuire's story because of his courage. I also tell it because it was at this conference where I found the book titled, *Healing the Trauma of Domestic Violence: A Workbook for Women* by Edward S. Kubany, Ph.D.; Mari A. Mc Caig, MSCP; and Janet Lacaonsay, MA, which shares powerful and helpful lessons regarding negative self-talk. I have modified the lesson somewhat for the purposes of this book.

EXERCISE: *Monitor Your Self-Talk*

Write your full name and the dates you intend to monitor. Let us start with two days. Be completely honest with yourself. First, you are going to become aware of making statements or phrases such as: "I should have ... " "I could have ... " or asking, "Why?" Why seems to be a big one. When I go through a crisis or am overcome, *why* is a biggie for me. Second, you are going to monitor your putdowns about your personality or character. Third, you are going to monitor "I feel" statements ending with words that are not emotions. Last, you are going to monitor apologies. I have problems to this day with that one. It is a process! Let us get started.

Day 1

Phrases or Comments

Time

Event or Circumstance

Day 2

Phrases or Comments

Time

Event or Circumstance

Here is what your log might look like.

Day 1

Monday

I could have been better prepared

I am going to ...

I feel so ...

Day 2

Tuesday

Why did I?

I am so stupid ...

I am so ...

Now, take those comments and phrases and dump them in the trash can. We all make mistakes. Sometimes there just isn't an answer. You need to accept that. You need to take control of your self-talk. Get back to the mirror. Give yourself a good, old pep talk. It's not stupid; it's self-preservation.

"Success is not a destination, it is a journey."
— John Wooden

A Piece of Me

Practice Makes Perfect

I will once again use the Miss Montana/Miss America system to help emphasize the technique. The main component that wins a pageant is consistency. The girl must look good physically and possess poise, talent, and intellect. The competition is divided into categories: swimsuit, talent, interview, and evening gown. In the interview, the girl is challenged on her ability to communicate intelligently, convey knowledge, have an opinion, be witty, and be approachable. These skills can only be gained if a girl knows herself. It requires hours of studying current events, learning to convey her opinions and convictions openly, logically, compassionately, intelligently, under the pressure of cameras, judges, and in some cases, audiences.

In the swimsuit competition, she is judged on her physical fitness and her ability to handle herself in an uncomfortable and unusual situation. Her ability to handle being on stage; appear natural, calm, and collected; along with tone and physical attractiveness are what earn her points in this portion of the competition.

The talent portion provides the contestant with the opportunity to demonstrate her talent, focus, competitiveness, communication skills, poise, motivation, self-confidence, discipline, likeability, and charisma.

The evening gown event provides the contestant with the opportunity to demonstrate her personal style, beauty, and grace. This is coupled with interview skills because the girls are asked a question publicly. The evening gown event provides the girl with the opportunity to pull it all together. This is usually the final phase of the competition, and this is her final opportunity to demonstrate the complete package. The girls realize that in order to win the crown, they must place consistently in the top ten percent in each category. Their marks need to be high and preferably among the top three. It is essential to be well-rounded. The whole package must exist. When we assess what creates a winner, we find self-confidence, self-belief, self-motivation, drive, discipline, and a positive attitude.

EXERCISE: *Practice Consistency*

Determine who and what it is that you want to become. Find someone who is doing what you want to do. Get them to coach you. Set a schedule. Practice the same time, the same day every week. Practice consistency. Imagine that you are the person that you want to be. If it is your dream to be a better basketball player, study the game, study the players, and practice, practice, and practice. If it is your dream to be a dancer, then practice, practice, and practice. Define your dream and practice consistency.

DATA DUMP

Please forgive me for:

I forgive myself for:

P.I.E.S.Reminder

"God's purpose may best be accomplished through our inactivity."
—Jane Rubietta

Chapter EIGHT

Emotional Baggage

Something to Think About:

"All psychological problems, from the slightest neurosis to the deepest psychosis, are merely symptoms of the frustration of fundamental need for a sense of personal worth. Self-esteem is the basic element in the health of any human personality."
—Dr. William Glasser

Date: _____
Today, I give thanks for

Signature: _____

A Piece of Me

You Can't Bury the Past

Feelings and emotions we think are long-forgotten can come back at any time. It happened to me after a mentally deranged former student cornered me in my classroom. Following that incident, I found myself haunted by my past. My emotions were out of control. I felt alone, anxious, ashamed, guilty, hopeless, overwhelmed, ugly, and unworthy. When I felt threatened, I had heart palpitations. I dreamed of being chased or assaulted, with flashbacks of past abusers.

I cleaned obsessively, purging my closest and my dresser drawers. I got rid of anything that reminded me of teaching, which I had loved. I stopped smiling. I lacked joy. I was isolated from friends and from doing activities I normally enjoyed.

I felt disconnected from those closest to me. It was difficult to concentrate, to sleep, and to eat. I was a mess. At times, I walked for hours. I felt numb. I'd tremble uncontrollably. I would only go outside if someone accompanied me. I felt cold. I dropped weight without trying. I didn't recognize myself. I felt out of control.

My skin turned gray, my legs gave out often, and I would fall on my snow-colored carpet. When I fell close to the bed, I would grab the covers tightly and pull my body up to a standing position. The paralysis would only last for a minute. Then I'd return to my daily routine. Sadly, part of that routine was lying in a fetal position on my bed with covers over my head to muffle the sounds of my crying. My clothing hung like drapery. I found my reflection repulsive, and a taste like that of a dirty ashtray made it difficult for me to eat.

Any loud sound startled me. My reactions were frightening. I'd lie hibernating in my bedroom with one sliver of light. I was afraid. I didn't know what was happening. I'd cry until there were no more tears. I'd see things. I was convinced that crows were haunting me. Evil surrounded me. I could feel it. I was scared, and I needed help. I prayed, and God put me in the hands of caring doctors.

"You are not crazy," they assured me. "You are suffering from PTSD (post-traumatic stress disorder). You have to open the box so you can move on."

I tried to keep it closed, but it didn't help. So I surrendered everything to God, and the memories rushed out like a roaring spring river. After I took back my senses, I realized I had forgotten that God was always with me. I began to understand that my emotions were normal reactions to extreme stress. My problems were the result of what happened to me, not because of anything I had done.

I learned from experience that many weight issues and eating disorders are the result of situations or circumstances beyond our control. It is up to us to find solutions to our problems and not run from them. Denial is dangerous! Life is full of surprises. It doesn't always go according to plan. Bad things happen. Parents divorce. Good, hard-working employees lose their jobs. Life requires that we dig deep and remember our goals and dreams.

That's where the original P.I.E.S formula can help.

Original P.I.E.S. Formula

    Desire
+ Motivation
+ Commitment
+ Flexibility
+ <u>Acceptance</u>
= Change

For most of my life, I followed that formula. But for a time, I let emotions take over. This enabled others to control and have power over me. It also influenced how I saw and felt about myself. It created havoc with my self-image and self-esteem, something I would have never allowed before workplace harassment.

Determined to get my life back, I had a good, old-fashioned come-to-Jesus conversation followed up with a prayer to God and request to the universe. It reminded me that pain must be managed, not stuffed in a box. This light-bulb moment prompted me to find the motivation to share what I learned about self-image, self-esteem, nutrition, fitness, eating disorders, and life.

Emotions can be managed. So can eating habits. It's not going to be easy. However, it can be done. It must be done. Before we enter the world of eating disorders, try to determine whether or not you use food to cope or use food to fuel.

Emotional Eating Self-Inventory

Circle or highlight the answer that fits you best.

I eat when I am bored.
(Often) (Sometimes) (Never)

I eat at social gatherings even when I am not hungry.
(Often) (Sometimes) (Never)

I eat so I will not offend others.
(Often) (Sometimes) (Never)

I eat when I am lonely.
(Often) (Sometimes) (Never)

I eat when I am upset.
(Often) (Sometimes) (Never)

I eat when I am disappointed.
(Often) (Sometimes) (Never)

I eat when I am angry with someone.
(Often) (Sometimes) (Never)

I eat when I feel anxious.
(Often) (Sometimes) (Never)

I eat when I am nervous.
(Often) (Sometimes) (Never)

I eat to relax.
(Often) (Sometimes) (Never)

I dislike weighing what I weigh but eat anyway.
(Often) (Sometimes) (Never)

I eat when I am physically hungry.
(Often) (Sometimes) (Never)

I eat instead of talking about my problems.
(Often) (Sometimes) (Never)

When someone ticks me off, I eat.
(Often) (Sometimes) (Never)

I eat to avoid confrontation.
(Often) (Sometimes) (Never)

I eat after someone says something mean to me.
(Often) (Sometimes) (Never)

There are times my eating is out of control.
(Often) (Sometimes) (Never)

Food gives me immediate gratification and comfort.
(Often) (Sometimes) (Never)

I eat three healthy meals and munch on a few healthy snacks throughout my day.
(Often) (Sometimes) (Never)

If I am upset or disturbed, I eat fast.
(Often) (Sometimes) (Never)

For each *often*, give yourself two points. For each *sometimes*, give yourself one point. For each *never*, give yourself a zero. If you scored between ten and thirty, it's likely that you are an emotional eater. If you scored higher than thirty, you need to acknowledge that you may have a serious problem. You need to start managing your eating and take care of your emotions.

Managing Your Relationship with Food

Management is difficult, especially when emotions are involved, which is usually the case. That's what makes us unique from other species. Good managers share the following qualities.

- Excellent interpersonal communication skills
- Realize basic human needs
- Demonstrate compassion
- Demonstrate empathy
- Follows policies, laws, and rules
- Abide by contracts
- Are positive and productive leaders
- Tend to the task
- Strive to achieve their goals
- Provide resources
- Minimize costs
- Maximize income
- Create happy and productive employees

What makes them successful? They are driven to be the best they can be. Good managers are focused. They are clear. They set goals. They understand the game of winning. The driving force behind them is once again:

> Desire
> \+ Motivation
> \+ Commitment
> \+ Flexibility
> \+ <u>Acceptance</u>
> = Change

What does this have to do with food and your relationship with food? Everything! Emotions are to be managed. Your relationship with food must be managed. You are the manager of your mind, body, and spirit. So why not utilize good management skills?

Throughout this section, you will be given the opportunity to enter people's lives and learn how an eating disorder has damaged their lives. They became bad managers of their minds, bodies, and spirits.

The world of eating disorders is heartbreaking. I worked in a downtown Portland, Oregon, weight-loss clinic. A medical team monitored the clients' blood pressure and ketosis levels daily. Dieters were restricted to 450–650 calories a day. Each client was weighed daily and required to keep a personal weight-loss record. The diet consisted of high protein (primarily chicken, turkey, and fish). Carbohydrates were limited to vegetables low in fat and starch, and fruits with low sugar and fat content. All clients received fifteen to twenty minutes of counseling daily. For the most part, the people who entered the clinic doors were morbidly obese. Meet Tammy.

Obesity: *Tammy*

At age nineteen, Tammy was morbidly obese. When she came to the clinic, she needed heart surgery, but the doctors would not even consider an operation until she lost at least 150 pounds.

Before she began a weight-reduction program, we had to find out Tammy's actual weight. That wasn't easy. Tammy's more than 450 pounds would not register on our scales. After exploring all options, we sent Tammy to the Portland Zoo to get an accurate reading. Humiliated, ashamed, and desperate she wanted to lose weight so badly, when she was told she had to go to the zoo, she only smiled and agreed.

As we got to know Tammy, we learned about her eating habits. While we consider a glass of milk a single serving, Tammy's single serving was a full gallon. For her, a serving of cookies was one or two packages. She knew what she was doing was bad for her and longed for the day when she could sit on the city bus and only use one seat.

Tammy's mother died when she was very young, so her father did the best he could do to fill her void. Unfortunately that was with food.

Back in 1981, little was said about morbid obesity. Today the National Institutes of Health (NIH) estimate that one third of our population (97 million Americans) is overweight. Between 5–10 million are morbidly obese.

The NIH considers a person obese if their weight is more than 20 percent higher than his or her ideal body weight. At that point, the person's weight begins to pose a health risk. Obesity becomes "morbid" when it significantly increases the risk of one or more obesity-related health conditions. Morbid obesity is a serious chronic disease, with symptoms that build slowly over an extended period of time.

Obesity can be linked to numerous medical conditions including higher rates of certain types of cancer. Studies by the NIH show that obese men are more likely to develop cancer of the colon, rectum, or prostate. Obese women are more likely to develop cancer of the gallbladder, uterus, cervix, or ovaries. Esophageal cancer has also been associated with obesity. Other diseases and health problems linked to obesity include: type 2 diabetes, high blood pressure/heart disease, dyslipidemia/high cholesterol, osteoarthritis of weight-bearing joints, depression, sleep apnea/respiratory problems, gastroesophageal reflux/heartburn, infertility, urinary stress incontinence menstrual irregularities, and lymphedema.

EXERCISE: *Are you eating to fill the void of loss?*

Do you see yourself in Tammy? Yes or No

Are you eating excessive amounts of food to fill the void? Yes or No

Do you know your caloric intake? Yes or No

Do you have health problems because of your overeating? Yes or No

If so, please list them.

If you have health problems, are you seeing a health care professional? Yes or No

List the professionals that are helping you.

If so, are you following their advice? Yes or No

What advice have they given you?

*Do not forget to do your positive self-talk.

Bulimics & Bingers: *Becky*

When overeating becomes a regular occurrence, that is defined as binge eating or compulsive eating. It is often accompanied by feelings of shame and secrecy. Becky is a perfect example. Everyone loves her.

Her parents boast about her accomplishments. She's thin. She's beautiful. She's smart. She's perfect. But for Becky, every day is a struggle trying to maintain that picture of perfection.

She has trouble concentrating on anything other than her weight. No one knows that she keeps her "perfect" body by binging and purging. "I eat in secret. I do it a lot. At McDonald's, I order two large Cokes, two large orders of fries, and two Big Macs." At home, she is filled with disgust as she looks at the "fat" girl in the mirror. So she turns on the water to hide the noise, puts a finger down her throat, and regurgitates it all.

Those with binge eating or compulsive eating disorders consume excessive amounts of food. A binge eater may eat 10,000–20,000 calories worth of food during a binge while a person following a healthy eating plan may eat between 1,200 to 2,000 calories a day. Binge-eating disorder comes with many behavioral and emotional signs and symptoms. Know the symptoms. The sooner they are faced, the easier the recovery.

BEHAVIORS, SIGNS & SYMPTOMS:

- Hiding or hoarding food
- Hiding empty food containers
- Eating alone
- Eating a large amount of food in a short period of time
- Eating even when full
- Feeling that eating is out of control
- Depression
- Anxiety

Bulimics & Bingers: *Tara*

After her parents divorced when she was six, Tara's life fell apart. She and her mother moved from place to place, depending on the men in her mother's life. She was raped when she was fourteen. Her life was one of constant change. She became a chameleon—changing her attitude, appearance, and personality to meet the expectations of everyone but herself.

Her low self-esteem never allowed her to believe what family and friends told her. She was beautiful and smart. Instead, she saw someone who was overweight and unworthy. She worried that everyone would discover the truth as she saw it. Tara felt guilty for not living up to others' expectations. That guilt led to thoughts of shame, sadness, anger, and hopelessness.

Binge eating made her feel better, but when she began gaining weight, she started purging. Sadly, that process also produced what she described as "a wonderful high." No one knew a thing, not even during the three months when she stopped eating altogether.

Tara hid the truth from everyone for seven years. Her life was out of control, but ironically, her bulimia gave her a feeling of control and even a sense of discipline. She followed every binge with a new weight-loss plan. She abused diet pills. When she paired pills with workouts, she would often pass out. Her heartbeat became irregular. She had panic attacks. Her life was so far out of control that she prayed that she would simply die.

When Tara sought treatment, she found out how well she had hidden her deadly secret. Her family and friends were surprised. Some were supportive. Others were angry and disappointed. She had to face the fact that their approval (or disapproval) could not define her life.

Treatment was not easy. She had to face her own demons and learn to deal with her emotions. She learned to be true to herself rather than seeking the approval of others. Most important, she rediscovered her faith. According to Tara, "Performing for others, trying to look good to others does not make me worthy. God gave me absolute worth. I cannot add to or can I take from that. His love is all I need, and it is not going anywhere."

Tara is home now, but every day brings challenges. She is always afraid that her eating disorder will reappear. In a way, that disorder is still ruling her life. It is always on her mind, affecting her decisions about food, exercise, and every facet of her daily life. Tara continues to tell herself that, "I am worth it and I can do it!"

Bulimia and binge eating can happen to anyone at any time. It happens to beautiful, talented, and intelligent adolescents, high school students, college women, and executives. It happens to men with promising futures, beautiful families, and sports stars. What we think we see in other people is not the entire picture. Secrets are kept hidden in the dark because the real issue is frightening; sharing that with people who see a "perfect" person is scary. Many consciously choose not to find treatment, and others simply have no idea they are suffering.

Pig Outs: *Madison*

I served as head resident for Widenhouse, a dorm at Rocky Mountain College, while my husband, Gary worked in an ophthalmology clinic. Even though the dorm was officially co-ed, most of the residents were girls. One of their leaders was Madison. She was slim with green eyes and beautiful red hair. She was president of student body, a gifted artist, and an honor student. She was a college dream. But Madison and her friends were engaging in some very dangerous behavior.

One fall day, the housekeeper knocked on our apartment door. She said she felt that she had to show me something that had been bothering her for several weeks. I walked with her to the laundry room where she asked me to try to lift a very full trash bag. It was very heavy, and the contents were soft and squishy. I untied the bag and looked inside. I gagged. We hurriedly tied the bag back up. "See those pizza boxes?" she said. "Yes." "Those pizza boxes come with this bag every Monday morning." We looked again and found a room number on the boxes. It was Madison's room.

Suspecting that this was a case of binge eating or bulimia, I immediately went to my apartment and called RimRock Foundation, a local treatment center for eating disorders. They advised me to hold a mandatory meeting for the girls in the dorm. The dean of students agreed.

During the meeting (which Madison did not attend), we learned that binging and purging was a Saturday night ritual. Sadly, many of these students were very unhappy about having their secrets exposed. In fact, the editor of the campus newspaper questioned why I should have the right to tell these young ladies how much they should or should not eat. How dare I try to save a life?

Some of the girls took our warning to heart. Others, including Madison, kept on binging and purging, but they kept their activities away from the dorm. A year later Madison collapsed on her dorm floor. Luckily, her life was saved, but I never knew if that was enough to scare her out of this very dangerous method of weight control.

Bulimia is characterized by binge eating, or continually consuming large amounts of high-calorie foods until one feels gorged or bloated. In some colleges, binge eating or "pig outs" have become a group practice much like "keggers." For 10 percent of the population engaging in this activity, it becomes an addictive cycle and progresses into the chronic illness called Bulimia (*Eating Disorders*, 1986).

If you come across signs like these, please do not hesitate to try to help. Somebody is in pain, fulfilling their actual emotions with excessive amounts of food and finishing with purging. I can't promise that it will be easy, but embrace the chance to create a positive change in someone's life.

BULIMIA WARNING SIGNS:

- Preoccupied with body shape and weight
- Negative body image
- Constant dieting
- Feeling that you can't control your eating behavior
- Eating to the point of discomfort
- Moodiness
- Depression
- Anxiety
- Guilt
- Anger
- Hopelessness
- Unresolved feelings or hidden stressors
- Burns on the lips and dominant hand
- Sores, scars, or calluses on knuckles or hands
- Unusual high usage of laxatives or diuretics
- Going to the bathroom after eating or during meals
- Running the water in the bathroom often so people can't hear vomiting
- Hoarding food
- Hiding wrappers or containers

PHYSICAL COMPLICATIONS:

- Menstrual irregularities
- Metabolic imbalances
- Gastrointestinal problems
- Kidney problems
- Tooth decay
- Brittle nails
- Thinning hair
- Complexion problems
- Fatigue

EXERCISE: *Do you see yourself in any of these women?*

If so, who?

What do you see? Explain.

Do you look in the mirror? Yes or No

Do you like what you see when you look in the mirror? Yes or No

Explain.

Is it possible you need medical help? Yes or No

What is holding you back from getting medical help? Explain.

Reread the scenarios and warning signs; highlight the words that best describe you. Then list them on the blanks provided.

*Do not forget to do your positive self-talk.

Chocoholic: *Nancy*

Nancy, an executive working in downtown Portland, Oregon, sees candy every day on her way to work. She has a weakness for chocolate. It makes her feel good. For that reason, she eats a piece every day before work. Over time, one piece of chocolate becomes two, and two becomes three. Gradually she notices she is putting on weight. She ignores the weight gain. Eventually Nancy's love of chocolate brings her to the weight-loss clinic. During counseling, Nancy tells how her one piece of candy became more than a pound a day. "I tell ya, sometimes I eat as much as five pounds. I do it unconsciously. Today, I caught myself. I looked at myself. I really looked at myself, and that's why I am here. I am addicted to chocolate."

Nancy's addiction overpowered her. When I counseled Nancy, little was known about chocoholics. Today, researchers at the University of Dundee, in Scotland, claim chocolate addicts "experienced negative effects following consumption of chocolate." The International Journal of Eating Disorders reports that chocolate addicts also tend to eat "more than twice as much chocolate as the nonaddicts" and are "significantly more depressed."

"People who are stressed out may find short-term relief from eating chocolate," psychological nutritionist Jurriaan Plesman says, "but this will aggravate depression and anxiety by a rebound reaction."

According to Plesman, it isn't hard to fall into a cycle of addiction that can lead to negative psychological effects. Because chocolate is high in sugar and fat, it creates a stress-relieving effect on the brain. According to a study conducted by researchers from UC San Francisco, stress can be linked to overeating foods like chocolate. "When you are hungry or under stress, stress hormones ... appear to enhance one's wanting or craving of palatable foods," says Norman Pecoraro, a neuroscientist at the University of California San Francisco and co-author of the study.

EXERCISE: *Does eating chocolate really make you feel good?*

Do you see yourself in Nancy? Yes or No

How much chocolate do you consume in a day?

How much chocolate do you consume in a week?

Do you eat your chocolate in secret? Yes or No

Is it possible you have a problem? Yes or No

Are you capable of eliminating or cutting down on your chocolate intake?

Do you use chocolate to help calm yourself when something is bothering you?

Do you try to solve your problems by binging on chocolate? Yes or No

Do you simply overindulge on chocolate? Yes or No

Is chocolate creating health problems? Yes or No

Explain:

*Do not forget to do your positive self-talk.

Starchaholic: *Sandy*

Sandy was a surgical nurse who checked herself into the clinic one day after she walked out of a surgery. Sandy craved starch. She claimed it calmed her. So she would secretly keep a box of cereal on the lower shelf of a surgical cart just outside the surgery doors. One day during surgery, she had a panic attack. She walked out of surgery, went to her cart, grabbed the cereal, and devoured the entire box within minutes. That's when she realized she had a serious problem. A problem that could have cost someone else his or her life. That day Sandy ended up in my office.

EXERCISE: *Does eating fatty, starchy foods really bring you comfort?*

Do you see yourself in Sandy? Yes or No

Do you eat chips or grab for starchy, fatty foods when you are disturbed or upset? Yes or No

Do you try to solve your problems by binging on starchy foods? Yes or No

*Seek help if you believe you have a problem.

Anorexic: Mary

I was first introduced to anorexia nervosa in 1982, while working for a weight-loss company. We finished a great workout, and I entered the locker room to shower. As I approached my locker, I noticed a young college student in tears. When I asked her what was wrong, she replied, "I just wish I could do this and feel good. I just wish that I could feel good again. I wish I could focus on my studies and not be consumed with food, with exercise, with gaining weight."

I was stunned. All I saw was a beautiful and intelligent young woman. I sat; I listened and convinced her to seek help.

The trophy case at Mary's high school commemorated her achievements. She was student body president, prom queen, and played three varsity sports. She also earned straight A's. But she still wanted to be better. Her future depended on it.

Desperate to get into a top school, she discovered there are thousands of other girls just like her. That's when she made a calculated decision. She needed to be number one, above average in something. She mapped out a plan to be the best—to be the best runner. She told herself, "All I have to do is beat Liz. She's the only one in the state who can defeat me. I need to cut my time. I need to be number one. I'll practice more. I'll train harder. I'll eat less. I need to be number one." In college, without that number-one spot, she still feels like a loser. Mary keeps telling herself, "I need to be perfect. I need to be."

The primary symptoms of anorexia nervosa are the same today as they were in the 1980s. The National Eating Disorders Association in 2005 expressed anorexia nervosa's four primary symptoms as: (1) Resistance to maintaining body weight at or above a minimally normal weight for age and height. (2) Intense fear of weight gain or being "fat" even though underweight. (3) Disturbance in the experience of body weight or shape, undue influence of weight or shape on self-evaluation, or denial of the seriousness of low body weight. (4) Loss of menstrual periods in girls and women post-puberty.

ANOREXIA WARNING SIGNS:

- Obsession with weight, food calories, fat grams, and dieting.
- Distorted or disturbed body image.
- Cuts out all sweets and fats from their diet.
- Fear of food.
- Severe weight loss.
- Hides weight loss by wearing baggy clothes.
- Skips meals.
- When he or she does eat, they take little bites and nibble.
- He or she is obsessed with the scale.
- Weighs him or herself two or three times a day.
- Excessive exercising or compulsive exercise.
- Moodiness.
- Depression.

- Sometimes paranoid denial of hunger.
- Eats foods in certain order.
- Rearranges food on plate.
- Withdrawal from usual friends and activities.
- Behaviors and attitudes regarding weight loss, dieting, and control of food are primary concern.

PHYSICAL COMPLICATIONS:

- Menstrual irregularities
- Metabolic imbalances
- Gastrointestinal problems
- Cardiac arrhythmia
- Kidney problems
- Cosmetic problems
- Brittleness of bones
- Death

EXERCISE: *Take an honest look at yourself.*

Do you see yourself in any of these women? Yes or No

Reread the preceding scenarios and warning signs; highlight the words that best describe you.

How will you avoid being a self-destructive perfectionist today?

Anorexic/Bulimic & the Excessive Exerciser: *Stacey*

Stacey was a popular high school student. But she was also a perfectionist, very competitive and a self-described control freak. When she couldn't control what was going on in her life, she controlled what she was putting in her body.

Hoping to make the cross-country team, she ran with team members every day. Even more than the sense of belonging she got from the team, she loved the extreme calorie burn. She ran and ran. Her weight dropped from a healthy 115 to 92 pounds.

Fearing a heart attack, the doctor recommended in-patient treatment. But her parents insurance wouldn't cover it, so they opted for outpatient treatment. Her father held her hand the entire way, through doctor's appointments, therapy sessions, meal planning, and the occasional walk if she gained weight that week.

But when she started college, she also started binging and purging. And she was sent home from college for medical reasons. Through the power of prayer, support, family, and friends, she was finally able to overcome her disorder.

Stacey is now a wife and mother of two. She says her husband reminds her every day how beautiful she is. She runs a successful childcare business, is a director of early childhood ministries, and has returned to school. And she now runs marathons. But she also realizes the dangers, saying, "I will always have an eating disorder, much like an alcoholic will always have a drinking problem, but I'm 'sober,' I'm healthy, and I love myself!"

Anorexic/Bulimic & the Excessive Exerciser: *Beth*

Her parents' divorce changed Beth's life. She was only eight and felt that it was all her fault. Her goal became to do anything and everything to make her parents happy again. Her dad and grandmother both commented about her eating habits and weight, so even at a young age, Beth associated weight with parental approval.

By sixth grade, her weight-loss lifestyle included hundreds of crunches every day. She constantly checked the size of her stomach and her weight and ate only enough to maintain energy. Her routine was the same through high school where she was involved in basketball, volleyball, and track. When she was cut from the volleyball team, she signed up for the cross-country team.

She became addicted to running. Running developed muscle mass, which increased her weight; she stopped weighing herself and based her self-worth on looks alone. The smaller her body and pant size, the better.

When recovery from leg surgery did not allow her to exercise, she became addicted to fiber. She ate up to half a bag of prunes at one time. Other times, she chose Metamucil bars. She made sure that she flushed out her insides to make up for the lack of exercise.

When she could run again, she continued to mix fiber and exercise. Her college life was centered around binging, purging, and exercise. With studying all day and exercising for hours, she had no time for a life. In fact, without exercise, she felt she simply couldn't focus.

Then she discovered triathlons. She joined the track club, master swim program, and biking group. She took cycling classes while still taking sports conditioning classes and long runs. She averaged thirteen hours a week exercising. Her diet was restricted to turkey, salsa, carrots, mustard, rice cakes, and dried fruit. And through it all, she continued to deny she had a problem.

It all took a toll on her body. With a variety of physical problems, she was told to stop running and simply cross-train. She lost it. She had been in therapy for two years but was still in denial. So, on advice of her therapist, her family admitted her to an eating disorder treatment center.

Her therapy began by treating an abandoned eight-year-old child of divorce. She finally understood that her need to "fix" things didn't allow her to grieve for her broken family. She began to realize that eating disorders fit hand in hand with OCD. She was obsessed with exercise and perfection. And if she did not reach perfection in every aspect of her life, she became so anxious she couldn't make logical decisions.

Even today, Beth has to work to understand her emotions. She now understands that her eating disorder made her focus on perfection. But she realizes that perfection cannot be about just the body.

Beth also credits a higher power with her recovery. "I was truly healed because of the Lord. No matter what I asked of him, he always provided. I now see clearly that my purpose in this life is not to be thin but to live the fullest life possible."

EXERCISE: *Why do you exercise?*

Do you see yourself in Stacey or Beth? Yes or No

Do like what you see when you look in the mirror? Yes or No

What do you like? Explain

What is your exercise routine?

How often do you exercise?

Stuffing: *Kate & Toni*

Kate is a friend of mine. While in high school, she was gang raped on a Native American reservation. Instead of being supportive, the people in her community blamed her. And she began blaming herself. She felt ashamed, guilty, degraded, and powerless. She distrusted herself and others. She became obsessed with safety and lost most of her self-confidence.

When she married, it was not a healthy relationship. Physical and mental abuse, along with the negative self-talk, helped to contribute to her unhealthy relationships with men and food.

The initial rape, lack of support, and an abusive relationship wreaked havoc on her life both physically and mentally. She became a binge eater. She still is.

Some binge-eating episodes last for only a few hours while others last for days. After a binge, she purchases the latest diet pill or diet program and joins a gym. She empties her kitchen cupboards and refrigerator of all sugar and fat. Then Kate goes to the grocery store and stocks up on Weight Watchers, Healthy Choice, and other popular frozen meals. It makes her feel in control. She's not, but it makes her feel that way. Even though her cupboards and refrigerator are filled with healthier foods and she's exercising, Kate has never dealt with the real issues. She continues to play the yo-yo game in her relationships with self, others, and food.

Toni experienced a similar problem. She was in her thirties, a career girl with about thirty pounds to lose. Toni stuck to her diet until she became close to her goal weight. Then she would plateau or begin to gain weight. She finally confessed that she had been raped years ago while at her target weight. She was afraid that she would be raped once again if she reached 130 pounds.

When she came close to her goal, she self-medicated with food and returned to her self-destructive weight game. Both women were unable to move forward because they had not dealt with their pent-up emotions. When we are in the midst of our traumas or deny their existence, we cannot resolve the issue.

Yo-Yo Syndrome: *Jennifer*

Jennifer was forty-nine when I met her at the center. Her weight problems began in high school. At home in front of her family, she ate nutritious and healthy foods. After school, she and her friends ate junk food.

When Jennifer began nursing school, life became more confusing and stressful. As her stress level increased, so did the numbers on the scale. Then she went on a diet. Shortly after losing the weight, she met and married her true love. Jennifer was not yet out of nursing school, but she finished her schooling as her husband finished his.

After college, Jennifer and her husband took jobs in another state, moving miles away from family and familiar settings. Then Jennifer became pregnant. Pregnancy was Jennifer's excuse to indulge in poor eating habits. She munched on chocolate and chips, ate two hamburgers instead of one, and drank two Cokes instead of one.

After the baby was born, Jennifer went on the latest fad diet. Losing weight this time took a little more effort, but she got the job done. Then, Jennifer and her family had to move to another state. Once again, when she left her familiar surroundings and friends, Jennifer reached for the comfort of junk food.

She made friends in her new location and was once again brave enough to step on the scale. She had gained 100 pounds! She tried the latest fad diet, only to find it more difficult to lose weight. Feeling like a failure and ashamed of her appearance, Jennifer found herself at the weight-loss center.

Here Jennifer was able to admit to herself that she ate for comfort. When she missed her friends, she used junk food to compensate. When she became comfortable again, she dieted. Jennifer learned that emotions were controlling her eating habits. She confronted her problems and learned to face the fears that were damaging her and contributing to her weight gain. Jennifer learned that the term for her actions was yo-yo dieter.

EXERCISE: *What are you avoiding?*

Do you feel any of these unwanted emotions?

Do you try to avoid similar thoughts or feelings?

Are you running from something?

Are you eating because you've experienced something so terrible that it is locked up in a box within you?

Chances are if you see yourself in any of these women you need help. Stop playing the Yo-Yo game and seek help.

EXERCISE: *Getting Real*

Is your pitcher empty? Yes or No

Explain:

Do you see any of these women in yourself? Yes or No

If you answered yes, write or list what you see. You may want to start a different journal for this.

Do you feel overburdened? Yes or No

If so, why?

EXERCISE: *Prioritize your obligations & commitments.*

Obligations   Commitments

Now, examine your obligations. Is it possible for you to cut some commitments and obligations out of your life? Yes or No

Which obligations or commitments can you pass on to someone else? Please list.

What can be gained if you eliminate some obligations and commitments from your life?

Do you eat on the go? Yes and No

Do you eat while driving? Yes or No

What do you eat when you are rushing around?

Do you take at least a thirty-minute lunch break? Yes or No

If no, why not? Explain.

Are you making excuses, or do you really have time?

Do you have me time? Yes or No

Would you like me time? Yes or No

Do you manage yourself or others?

What is one thing you would do daily for yourself if you allowed yourself to omit one obligation or commitment?

*Take action and omit one obligation or commitment that will not cause harm to you or others. Now, take that time and use it for yourself.

Are you making progress? Yes or No

Baby & Belly Fat: *Clients*

Working for a weight-loss company, I noticed that many of the women I counseled carried extra weight around their bellies, weight they acquired while pregnant. Most of these women found pregnancy to be a time of joy. Most of these women also found it difficult to let go of their belly fat where baby once lived. When counseling these women, I noticed how they held their bellies, rested their hands on their bellies, and guarded their bellies with items like purses, coats, etc. It was as if they were protecting themselves. I began to wonder if this was somehow a way of holding on to something that was taken from them. Did most of these women only feel loved while pregnant? I asked some of them, and they admitted their fat gave them a protective shield.

EXERCISE: *Are you using belly fat for a protective shield?*

Why are you holding onto the baby fat around your middle?

Does your fat make you feel secure? Yes or No

Is your fat an excuse to hold on to something that once lived within you? Yes or No

Do you feel empty inside? Yes or No

Are you filling your void or emptiness with fat? Yes or No

Is your fat protecting you? Yes or No

Is your baby belly fat keeping you from intimacy? Yes or No

What are you getting by holding on to your fat around the middle?

EXERCISE: *Wrap-Up Questions*

Are you eating and purging your emotions unhealthily?

Do you excuse yourself from the real issue or issues?

If so, how?

Are you a good advocate for yourself? Yes or No

Explain:

Do you feel guilty when you put yourself first or do for yourself? Yes or No

Do you feel selfish when you do for yourself? Yes or No

Are you willing to become your own self-advocate? Yes or No

Are you willing to begin to understand the need for positive self-talk? Yes or No

What are three negative things you tell yourself?

What are six positive things you tell yourself? Try to include all aspects of P.I.E.S. (physical, intellectual, emotional, spiritual). Be honest!

*A person's character determines how others view your attitudes, moral conscience, feelings, and concerns. It also is how we see others and their outlooks on life.

EXERCISE: *Character Analysis*

How do you see yourself? How do others see you? This includes your spiritual leaders and or God. Circle or highlight words in each category that apply to you. Then write a character analysis describing how you want to be perceived. Then take the time to write out how you are going to become this person. Imagine and create.

WORDS THAT EXPRESS EMOTIONS

Aggressive	Exhausted	Miserable
Aggravated	Fearful	Optimistic
Alienated	Frightened	Paranoid
Angry	Frustrated	Peaceful
Annoyed	Guilty	Proud
Anxious	Happy	Puzzled
Apathetic	Helpless	Regretful
Bashful	Hopeful	Relieved
Careful	Happy	Sad
Cautious	Helpless	Satisfied
Confident	Hostile	Shocked
Curious	Humiliated	Shy
Depressed	Hurt	Sorry
Determined	Hysterical	Sure
Disappointed	Innocent	Surprised
Discouraged	Interested	Suspicious
Disgusted	Jealous	Thoughtful
Ecstatic	Lonely	Undecided
Embarrassed	Loved	Withdrawn
Enthusiastic	Love struck	
Envious	Mischievous	

WORDS THAT EXPRESS FEELINGS

Accepting	Considerate	Loser	Serene
Absorbed	Courageous	Lousy	Shaky
Admiration	Gay	Loved	Shocked
Affected	Glad	Love Struck	Sorry
Affectionate	Gleeful	Loving	Spirited
Afflicted	Graceful	Luscious	Snoopy
Aggravated	Grateful	Lucky	Sunny
Aggressive	Gratuitous	Mournful	Surprised
Alienated	Great	Merry	Sure
Alone	Guilty	Mindful	Suspicious
Amazed	Happy	Mischievous	Sympathetic
Ambitious	Helpless	Miserable	Tender
Angry	Honored	Nervous	Thankful
Animated	Hopeful	Nosy	Thoughtful
Annoyed	Hostile	Optimistic	Threatened
Anxious	Humiliated	Offended	Thrilled
Apathetic	Hurt	Original	Timid
Appreciated	Hysterical	Overjoyed	Unappreciated
Ashamed	Important	Panicked	Uncertain
Attractive	Incapable	Paralyzed	Undecided
At ease	Innocent	Paranoid	Understanding
Bashful	Innocent	Passionate	Unhappy
Beautiful	Indecisive	Passionately	Unique
Blessed	Isolated	Pessimistic	Upset
Bold	Insulted	Peaceful	Victimized
Brave	Intrigued	Playful	Vibrant
Bright	Interested	Pleased	Weary
Calm	Irritated	Preoccupied	Withdrawn
Careful	Keen	Perplexed	Wonderful
Cautious	Kind	Prideful	Worried
Certain	Jealous	Proud	Worthless
Challenged	Joyful	Provocative	Worthy
Cheerful	Joyous	Puzzled	Wronged
Clever	Jubilant	Relaxed	
Comfortable	Liberated	Quiet	
Concerned	Lifeless	Reassured	
Confident	Lively	Rebellious	
Conflicted	Lonely	Sensitive	

DESCRIBING WORDS

- Abundant
- Accepting
- Accurate
- Adventurous
- Affectionate
- Alert
- Altruistic
- Ambitious
- Amiable
- Annoying
- Antagonistic
- Anxious
- Appealing
- Arrogant
- Attractive
- Athletic
- Average
- Awkward
- Beautiful
- Beautiful hair
- Beautiful hands
- Biased
- Boastful
- Bony
- Book-smart
- Brave
- Bright
- Bright-eyed
- Cantankerous
- Capable
- Careful
- Caring
- Charitable
- Charming
- Cheerful
- Chic
- Clever
- Comfortable
- Compassionate
- Compatible
- Complaining
- Conceited
- Confident
- Conscientious
- Conservative
- Considerate
- Cordially
- Courageous
- Creative
- Curios
- Cute
- Daring
- Deceitful
- Delightful
- Disheveled
- Desirable
- Determined
- Dishonest
- Discriminating
- Ecstatic
- Eager
- Egotistical
- Elegant
- Empathic
- Encouraging
- Energetic
- Enthusiastic
- Envious
- Exaggerator
- Exciting
- Extroverted
- Faithful
- Feminine
- Flexible
- Forgiving
- Fortunate
- Friendly
- Fruitful
- Frugal
- Fun
- Generous
- Gentle
- Gifted
- Giving
- Gorgeous
- Gracious
- Great
- Great legs
- Happy
- Harmonious
- Hateful
- Helpful
- Honorable
- Honest
- Hospitable
- Humble
- Humane
- Humorous
- Independent
- Informative
- Inspirational
- Inspired
- Insightful
- Intelligent
- Interesting
- Intriguing
- Introverted
- Inventive
- Jealous
- Joyful
- Kind
- Kind hearted
- Knowledgeable
- Lanky
- Lazy
- Likable
- Lonely
- Loving
- Mannerly
- Masculine
- Mindful
- Miserly
- Moderate
- Muscular
- Naughty
- Neat
- Negative
- Nice
- Nice-looking
- Normal
- Observant
- Old
- Old-looking
- Open
- Open-minded
- Opinionated
- Optimistic
- Ordinary
- Passionate
- Patient
- Patriotic
- Peaceful
- Peppy
- Pessimistic
- Perfectionist
- Persistent
- Personable
- Pleasant
- Polite
- Positive
- Precise
- Prejudicial
- Private
- Productive
- Prosperous
- Proud
- Purposeful
- Qualified
- Quaint
- Quick
- Quick-tempered
- Quiet
- Reasonable
- Reliable
- Resourceful
- Respectful
- Responsible
- Religious
- Rich
- Righteous
- Rude
- Salty
- Savvy
- Selfish
- Selfless
- Self-motivated
- Sensible
- Serious
- Silent
- Sincere
- Skilled
- Smart
- Solid
- Spiritual
- Strong
- Stubborn
- Stupid
- Supportive
- Sweet
- Sympathetic
- Under qualified
- Unique
- Tactful
- Talented
- Tenacious
- Tender
- Thrifty
- Thoughtful
- Trustful
- Truthful
- Warm
- Warm-hearted
- Wealthy Wise
- Witty
- Zealous
- Zestful

DATA DUMP

Please forgive me for:

I forgive myself for:

                        P.I.E.S. Reminder

"The love of God surrounds us
Like the air we breathe around us,
As near a heartbeat, as close as a prayer,
And whenever we need Him, He'll always be there!"
—Helen Steiner Rice

NINE

Simply Put, Knowledge Is Power

Something to Think About:

> "Get the facts first, and then you can distort 'em as you please."
> —Mark Twain

Date: _____
Today, I give thanks for

Signature: _____

Simply Put

We would all like to fit into the "gold standard" for our weight. However, our weight can be deceiving. Your primary concern should be your health and performance levels. Body-fat percentage is what you should be most concerned with as high levels of fat may lead to health issues.

Scales can be deceiving. They do not always represent an honest picture. I suggest you track your waist size. This will allow you to see results not reflected on the scale. Decreasing waist sizes generally equal bad adipose (fat) tissue reduction. As you gain lean tissue (muscle), your metabolism gets a boost. An efficient metabolism makes it easier to work out and lose weight. You gain more energy and feel better! Although scales can be deceiving, they are a valuable tool in the weight-loss game. For this reason, I have supplied you with a guide.

Weight Standard for Women

The chart below is divided into small, medium, and large. This represents frame size. The best way to determine frame size is to measure the width of your shoulders and hips and measure your wrists and ankles. Those with narrow shoulders and hips and small wrists and ankles are considered small framed. Those with wide shoulders and hips and large wrists and ankles are considered large. Most of us fit into the medium-frame category.

Height	Small Frame	Medium Frame	Large Frame
4'9"	99–108	106–118	115–128
4'10"	100–110	108–120	117–131
4'11"	101–112	110–123	117–131
5'0"	103–115	112–126	121–137
5'1"	105–118	115–129	125–140
5'2"	108–121	118–132	128–144
5'3"	111–124	121–135	131–148
5'4"	114–127	124–138	134–152
5'5"	117–130	127–141	137–156
5'6"	120–133	130–144	140–160
5'7"	123–136	133–147	143–164
5'8"	126–139	136–150	146–167
5'9"	129–142	139–153	149–170
5'10"	132–145	142–156	152–173
5'11"	135–148	145–159	155–176

Source: ®American Medical Association.

We can get obsessive about our weight. If this happens to you, use the "favorite pants" method. It's not scientific, but it does work. We all have that one pair of jeans or slacks that we love. When they fit well, we feel great. Your goal should be to fit in those pants again.

My Food Plate

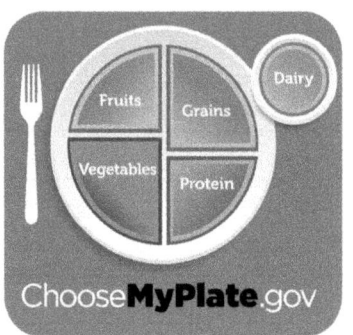

In 2011, the USDA released MyPlate.gov, a new concept to convey basic information about healthy eating. I prefer the pyramid because it reminds us to be active rather than concentrate on just what's on the plate.

The Food Pyramid

The Food Pyramid is the revised dietary guideline of 2005, which was released by the United States Department of Agriculture (USDA). The five food groups: grains (orange), vegetables (green), fruit (red), milk/dairy (blue), and meat and beans (purple). It represents a well-balanced healthy lifestyle. Concepts to improve the overall well-being of Americans.

The areas of the colors on the pyramid are positioned to represent each food group's daily recommended amount. The smaller top portion where the colors collide signifies the categories with little or no saturated fats and sugars, and the wider widths exemplify foods with those substances. Here are the recommended daily proportions:

- Grains: 5–8 oz
- Vegetables: 2.5–3 C
- Fruits: 1.5–2 C
- Milk/Dairy: 3 C
- Meat/Beans: 5–6 oz

The person climbing the stairs on the pyramid represents the importance of daily activity that should be incorporated to improve the well-being of a person's life. The narrowing of the colors from bottom to top symbolizes moderation of foods, and the base signifies proportionality; variety is symbolized by the different colors. The pyramid is a great guideline for those "stepping toward a healthier you!"

To determine your individual needs, go to the website mypyramid.gov where you can personalize your diet by entering your age, gender, activity level, and goals. This is a great tool to get your healthy ways in progress.

Food Labels

How do I read a food label?

If you want to be healthy, lose weight, or maintain your weight, you must educate yourself and learn to read labels.

Nutrition Facts	
Serving Size 1 cup (228g) Servings Per Container 2	Start here
Amount Per Serving	
Calories 250 Calories from Fat 110	Check calories
% Daily Value*	Quick guide to % DV
Total Fat 12g — 18% Saturated Fat 3g — 15% *Trans* Fat 3g	5% or less is low 20% or more is high
Cholesterol 30mg — 10% **Sodium** 470mg — 20% **Potassium** 700mg — 20%	Limit these
Total Carbohydrate 31g — 10% Dietary Fiber 0g — 0% Sugars 5g **Protein** 5g	Get enough of these
Vitamin A — 4% Vitamin C — 2% Calcium — 20% Iron — 4%	Footnote

	Calories	2,000	2,500
Total Fat	Less than	65g	80g
Sat Fat	Less than	20g	25g
Cholesterol	Less than	300mg	300mg
Sodium	Less than	2,400mg	2,400mg
Total Carbohydrate		300g	375g
Dietary Fiber		25g	30g

*Percent Daily Values are based on a 2,000 calorie diet. Your Daily Values may be higher or lower depending on your calorie needs.

SERVING SIZE

All the numbers above are based on serving size. They typically contain familiar units like a cup(s) or a count and are followed by the metric unit in grams. It is important to know the serving size as well as how many serving sizes are contained in the package or food item. It is even more important to know how much you actually consume. In this example, one serving size prepared is 1 cup, which is equal to 228 grams and 250 calories. There are two servings in this container.

AMOUNT OF CALORIES PER SERVING

This section will tell you how much energy you are getting by eating one serving of the product. In this example, one serving equals 250 calories.

*Use these guidelines when you are shopping:

- Low caloric: 40 cals
- Moderate: 100 cals
- High caloric: $>=$ 400 cals

CALORIES FROM FAT PER SERVING:

This section is very important for those losing weight and those concerned about their overall health. High fat servings can halt weight loss and increase the risk of obesity, therefore increasing the risk of cardiovascular disease and other health issues. No more than 35 percent of your daily caloric intake should be from fat. If you are trying to lose weight, eat no more than 20 percent. To find the percentage of fat per serving, divide the calories from fat by 100.

Do not confuse the calories from fat number with the percentage, which is discussed next. Aim for products that include no more than 20–35 percent of fat, and preferably of unsaturated fat.

% DAILY VALUE (%DV):

There is a recommended daily amount for each nutrient. The percentage shown represents how well the product meets that recommended amount (based on a 2000-calorie diet). These daily values are often found at the bottom of the nutrition fact label and are listed below for your reference. You will see that some nutrients are labeled to eat "less than" and the other two, total carbohydrates and fiber, are suggesting you eat "at least" that amount daily.

Let's look at an example of each:

The upper limit for cholesterol is 300 mg. Consuming less than that is preferred. One large egg contains about 210 mg, or 70 percent of the daily amount. The DV for fiber is 25 g. Eating two servings of macaroni and cheese only meets 8 percent of that amount. That means that you have 92 percent more fiber to eat throughout the day. (Remember you have already consumed 820 cals!) If your dietary needs are more or less than 2000, you can still use the %DV to determine whether or not a product is high or low in a particular nutrient. A good rule of thumb is items <5 %DV is low of that nutrient (good reference for total fat, saturated fat, sodium, and cholesterol), and >20% is high of that nutrient.

%DV can also be used to compare items. Let's compare the fat content in a single serving, in this case 1 cup, in 2% milk and nonfat milk by using the %DV column. The %DV for milk in 2% milk is as follows:

- Total Fat: 8%
- Sat Fat: 15%
- Now look at nonfat skim milk:
- Total Fat: 0%
- Sat Fat: 0%

If you compare these items yourself, the calcium content is the same, so you are not missing anything but unwanted fat! Using the percentage column is a good tool to decrease fats and sodium in your diet and to choose products with a better source of fiber and vitamins.

If you consume more or less than 2000 calories, the %DV will have to be adjusted according to your dietary needs but can still be used as a reference.

RECOMMENDED DAILY VALUES (DV)

Calories		2,000	2,500
Total Fat	Less than	65 g	85 g
Sat Fat	Less than	20 g	25 g
Cholesterol	Less than	300 mg	300 mg
Sodium	Less than	2400 mg	2400 mg
Total Carbohydrate		300 g	375 g
Dietary Fiber		25 g	30 g

Notice that transfat, sugars, and protein do not have percentages. There is a good reason for that. Transfat should be eliminated from the diet completely because of its health risks. There is no recommendation for sugar needed in one day. Remember that there are natural sugars in milk, fruits, and vegetables. Protein does not need a %DV unless it is making a claim such as a "high protein" product.

SIMPLY PUT

- Take the time to read food labels of foods you are eating.
- Learn how to read them and pay close attention to the amount of calories per serving as well as the fat content.
- Knowledge is power. Reading labels can equal a healthier you.

Glycemic Index

SIMPLY PUT

The majority of carbohydrates consumed should be low glycemic because they take longer to digest. Therefore, energy is released at a slower rate taking a longer period of time. Weight management assists in controlling insulin levels and contributes to longer endurance performance. High glycemic foods should be limited. Quick spikes in sugar from many high glycemic processed sources, such as white bread, candy, and soda that are not used up immediately, are easily stored as fat.

LOW GLYCEMIC FOODS

- Apples
- Artichokes
- Asparagus
- Broccoli
- Carrots
- Cauliflower
- Celery
- Chickpeas
- Cucumbers
- Fructose (natural sugar found in fruits and vegetables)
- Green beans
- Kidney beans
- Low-fat yogurt
- Low-fat milk
- Multi grain bread
- Oranges
- Pears
- Plums
- Skim milk
- Tomatoes
- Whole grain bread and cereals
- Whole wheat pasta
- Lettuce

BETTER CHOICES OF MEDIUM-HIGH GLYCEMIC FOODS

- Baked potatoes
- Bananas
- Couscous
- Orange juice
- Pineapples
- Popcorn
- Pretzels
- Raisins
- Rice cakes
- Sweet potatoes
- Watermelon

Calories

SIMPLY PUT

A calorie is how we measure energy from food. Each macronutrient—fat, carbohydrates, and protein—provide us with energy:

Fat: 9 cals per gram
Carbohydrates: 4 cals per gram
Protein: 4 cals per gram

1 pound=3,500 calories so to lose 1 pound you must burn 3,500 calories. The best way is to lose is to cut your caloric intake and amp up your exercise. When I am trying to lose weight, I eat between 900–1200 calories per day. Some professionals suggest not going below 1400. Burning calories is vital. Try burning at least 200-300 to hundred calories during your workout. There is nothing magical about losing weight. Calories in must be burned. It's that simple.

Breakfast

SIMPLY PUT

Breakfast is the most important meal of the day. Your body has been fasting for over eight hours and is craving energy. More importantly, your brain is yearning for glucose. It is essential to refuel your brain. Think about it. On the days you skipped out on breakfast, do you feel sluggish and find it hard to focus? How about the days you do begin your day with oatmeal, yogurt and granola, or whole-wheat pancakes?

My bet is that you feel energized and more attentive as you begin your day. Breakfasts with high fiber, protein, and whole-wheat carbohydrates will keep you feeling full longer and keep you from reaching for unnecessary snacks throughout the day. Oh yeah, did I mention that it might help slim your waistline?

Carbohydrates

Will carbohydrates (CHO) make me fat?

Weight gain occurs when energy intake is greater than energy output. Moderation is key. According to food pyramid guidelines, 45–65 percent of total calories should be from carbohydrates. The Recommended Dietary Allowance (RDA) recommends at least 130 grams of CHO/day specifically to meet the minimum needed for brain functioning. The specific amount depends greatly on your activity level and the goals you wish to achieve. Carbohydrates provide the body with immediate and sustained energy. Short bursts of activity up to three minutes can be performed without the use of oxygen, and this stored fuel in the muscle comes from glucose (anaerobic metabolism). Beyond that time, aerobic metabolism (the use of oxygen) is necessary for activities of longer duration since it can produce a large amount of ATP (energy). Without this fuel source, the brain is deprived and activity level and duration decrease. If your goal is to lose weight, do not completely skip your carbs.

Consider the better choices of CHOs. There are two types of carbohydrates, simple and complex. Simple carbohydrates, or simple sugars, are sugars that contain one single molecule (monosaccharide) or two combined (disaccharides). Simple sugars, like fructose (found in fruit), lactose (in milk), and glucose (most common form of energy) as well as combined forms are digested rather speedily and can be used as immediate energy. If intake of simple sugars exceeds the amount used instantly, it will usually be stored as fat.

This does not mean that eating fruit is going to increase your fat storage. Even though fructose is the sweetest-tasting sugar and is used to artificially flavor many candies, jellies, and sodas in the form of high fructose corn syrup (HFCS), it is found naturally as well. Natural sugars, those found in fruit and some vegetables, are the best sugars to eat, as they are rich in carbohydrates, high in fiber, and contain no "empty" calories. Many contain vitamin C, potassium, and carry antioxidants that help fight off free radicals (ACSM). Refined sugars can still be enjoyed but should be used sparingly. Instead of reaching for apple pie after dinner, enjoy a yogurt parfait with berries to satisfy your sweet tooth.

The other most efficient fuel source is complex carbohydrates made up of sugars composed of several chains and complicated structures. These consist of starches found in plants, glycogen found in animals, and fiber, which is not digested at all. Because of their intricate design and fiber dosage, complex carbohydrates are digested more slowly and are a greater fuel source.

When choosing carbohydrates for your diet, it is important to select the most nutrient-dense carbohydrates. The richest source comes from a variety of fruits, vegetables, and whole grains. For those wanting to lose weight, fruits and vegetables are best because they are typically lower in calories, but they do not provide as much energy as whole grains. Fruits and vegetables are found in many forms, making them easily accessible. Of course, there are greater benefits to some forms than others.

Fresh fruits and vegetables are obviously ideal but are not realistic in more isolated areas, and they age quickly. Frozen and canned fruits and vegetables retain most of the nutrients and can be used in a variety of ways. However, when purchasing canned produce, it is important to look for fruits canned in their own juice, not additional sweeteners, and vegetables should be rinsed before use to wash out added preservatives. Dried fruits and vegetables are typically high in calories and are not the preferred form. They may be included during activities, such as hiking, or in other instances when fresh produce is not available. Moderate amounts of juices are good sources of vitamins and minerals in a concentrated fashion.

Whole grains are a great source of complex carbohydrates as they contain rich amounts of fiber and vitamin B. Fiber provides no nutrients but slows down digestion, making you feel full longer. When buying whole grain foods, whole wheat or whole grain should be the first ingredient on the list. If not, it probably contains burnt sugar or molasses, giving it a darker color, causing you to think it is the better choice. Read the labels; just because the big print reads "wheat" does not mean the product is whole wheat! Check the fine print. Refined grains contain fewer vitamins and minerals and should be consumed moderately. Good sources of whole grain food include whole wheat bread, cereals, crackers, pastas, and oatmeal.

SIMPLY PUT

Best Choices:

- Beans
- Fresh fruit
- Legumes
- Raw vegetables
- Steamed vegetables
- Unsalted nuts
- Unsalted seeds
- Whole grain
- Whole wheat

Here is a more detailed list. You will also find these foods on your grocery list and many of the same foods on the reduction list.

VEGETABLES

Alfalfa sprouts	Chinese cabbage	Potatoes
Artichoke	Collard	Scallops
Arugula	Corn	Snow peas
Asparagus	Cucumber	Shallots
Avocados	Dandelion green	Snow peas
Bamboo shoots	Endive	Spinach
Bean sprout	Eggplant	Squash
Beet greens	Green beans	Tomatoes
Bok choy	Kohlrabi	Turnips
Broccoli	Lettuce	Turnip greens
Cabbage	Mushrooms	Watercress
Carrots	Mustard greens	Wax beans
Cauliflower	Okra	Yard long beans
Celery	Onion	Yellow beans
Chard	Peppers (all kinds)	Zucchini
Chicory	Pickles	

(Notice I put tomatoes in the vegetable section. I also list them in fruit. Tomatoes are a fruit, but many of us recognize them as a vegetable.)

FRUITS

Apples	Fig	Papaya
Apricots	Gooseberry	Passion fruit
Asian pears	Mulberry	Peaches
Bananas	Grapefruit	Pears
Blackberry	Grapes	Persimmons
Blueberry	Guava	Pineapple
Boysenberry	Honeydew	Plums
Cantaloupe	Kiwi	Pomegranate
Casaba	Kumquat	Raspberry
Cherries	Lemon	Star fruit
Crabapple	Lime	Strawberry
Cranberry	Mangoes	Tangerines
Crenshaw	Mandarins	Tomatoes
Currant	Nectarines	
Elderberry	Oranges	

BREADS & CEREALS

Ak-Mak crackers	Melba toast	Shredded wheat
Bran cereals low in sugar	Norwegian flatbread	Special K
		Wasa crisp crackers
Finn crisp crackers	Oatmeal	Whole wheat
Hollywood (brown)	Pita bread	Zoom
Italian breadsticks	Puffed rice	

NUTS & SEEDS

Almonds	Macadamia nuts	Pumpkin seeds
Cashews	Peanuts	Sunflower seeds
Chestnuts	Pistachios	Walnuts
Coconut		

BEANS & LEGUMES

Black-eyed peas	Lentils	Pinto
Garbanzo beans	Lima	Split peas
Kidney beans	Navy	White beans

Sugar & the Oses

Does fruit or fructose make you fat?

First, what is fructose? It is a simple sugar, which is a type of carbohydrate. It is actually a low-glycemic carbohydrate found in natural foods. In addition to fructose, the other two simple sugars that provide nutrients are glucose and sucrose. They are monosacharides, meaning a single molecule of sugar. In particular, fructose provides the sweetest taste and is naturally produced in fruits and used as artificial flavoring to many candies, jellies, and sodas in the form of high fructose corn syrup (HFCS). As a natural sugar, fructose found in fruit and some vegetables is the best sweetener to eat, since it is carbohydrate rich, high in fiber, and lower in calories. Many fruits and veggies also contain vitamin C, potassium, and carry antioxidants that help fight off free radicals (can damage cells and lead to diseases such as cancer). Refined sugars can still be enjoyed, but use them sparingly.

SIMPLY PUT

Fructose eaten in its natural form through fruits and vegetables is the best form of sugar to consume. These foods are high in fiber, low in calories, and may offer health benefits. Eating natural fructose can satisfy your sweet tooth craving and make you feel full without guilt because of its low calorie content. Do not mistake high fructose corn syrup (HFCS) with natural fructose. HFCS is found in candies, sodas, jams, and other processed foods that quickly spike the blood sugar and is easily converted to fat if not immediately used.

BEWARE OF SUGARY WORDS

- Corn syrup
- Dextrose
- Fructose
- Fruit juice concentrate
- High fructose Corn syrup (HFCS)
- Honey
- Maltose
- Maple syrup
- Sucrose

FRUITS LOW IN SUGAR

- Blackberries
- Cranberries
- Papaya
- Peaches
- Raspberries
- Small amounts of lemon or lime
- Strawberries
- Tomatoes

VEGETABLES LOW IN SUGAR

- Broccoli
- Cauliflower
- Mushrooms
- Raw or cooked carrots
- Rhubarb

Insulin & Fat

What role does insulin play in the storing of fat?

Insulin is a hormone that is released from the pancreas after a meal or snack. Its role is to control carbohydrate metabolism and blood glucose dumping to lower the blood glucose levels (ACSM). Once food is eaten, glucose levels are elevated, resulting in the release of insulin to decrease the amount of sugar floating around in the blood. Carbohydrates are ingested to refuel liver and muscle glycogen, but liver glycogen is the only accessible source that can be used for the brain and keep glucose levels balanced. If the energy source is not immediately taken up by the muscles or if liver glycogen is too full, carbohydrates are turned into fat. Refined sugars spike insulin levels more than nutrient-dense complex carbohydrates, making it difficult to use stored fat for energy. High insulin levels suppress glucagon, which is a hormone used to help burn sugar and fat (http://rheumatic.org/insulin.htm). So for those trying to lose weight, controlling insulin levels is important.

SIMPLY PUT

You can moderate the secretion of insulin by consuming nutrient-dense carbohydrates, keeping the amount of carbohydrates to the minimum of 45 percent of your daily caloric intake, and limiting the amount of refined sugars.

NUTRIENT-DENSE CARBOHYDRATES

- Whole wheat bread, cereal, and pasta—if your caloric intake is 1200 calories, the consumption of carbohydrates should be 540 calories or 135 grams.

- Refined sugar has been put through a process that loses the purity of all nutrients.
- Sugar from sugar cane and sugar beets are taken and put through several processes to increase their life and sweetness.
- Sugar is considered as "empty calories" with no nutritional value.
- Sugar also eats away at your gums and enamel, so listen to your dentist when he says cut the sugar!

Prebiotics & Probiotics

SIMPLY PUT

Prebiotics are certain fiberlike forms of indigestible carbohydrates that support growth of beneficial bacteria in the lower intestine.

PREBIOTICS

Chicory	Garlic
Jerusalem artichokes	Leeks
Wheat	Prebiotic tablets, powders, and
Rye	nutritional beverages.
Onions	

Probiotics are strains of lactobacillus and bifdobacteria that have beneficial effects on the body. Also called "friendly bacteria."

PROBIOTICS

Fermented or aged milk or milk products
Yogurt
Buttermilk
Kefir
Cottage Cheese

Other fermented products
Soy sauce
Fresh sauerkraut
Probiotic tables, and powders and nutritional beverages

Wheat

Does wheat make you fat?

Wheat is a complex carbohydrate, a nutrient-dense component of a healthy diet. Compared to refined grains, whole wheat is the best form to eat because it offers the greatest amount of nutrients, as well as longest sustaining energy (ACSM). Wheat will not make you fat as long as you keep a balanced energy equation. Eating a balanced diet with the inclusion of carbohydrates is necessary for sustaining a healthy lifestyle. For those who want to lose weight, eating a plentiful amount of fruits and vegetables in addition to some whole-grain products to meet the carbohydrate daily needs is a viable choice.

SIMPLY PUT

- The best diet contains a variety and a moderate amount of whole grain foods—along with fruits, vegetables, dairy, and meat/legumes.
- Eating only wheat or carbohydrates and/or eating in excess will cause weight gain.
- When eating wheat, choose whole wheat for best nutritional content; be aware of the amount of servings you are consuming.

EXAMPLES OF 1 OZ. GRAIN CHOICES:

1 slice whole grain
1 C whole grain cereal
1/2 C whole grain rice
1 C oatmeal
3 C popcorn

Fat

Should I cut all fat from my diet?

Fat storage in significant amounts can cause health problems. Heart disease is the number one killer in the United States. Having excess fat, especially around the abdomen, as well as high blood pressure, high cholesterol, diabetes, and smoking will increase the risk (cdc.gov). As we said before, it is not eating fats that make you fat, but eating more required to provide the energy your body uses. However, if you are trying to lose weight, eating less fat consuming more nutritional foods within your caloric limit will most likely provide better results.

SIMPLY PUT

Choose moderation when snacking. Moderation means having one cookie, one slice of cake, a scoop and a half of ice cream, a handful of chips, a slice of a favorite pizza, or a cheeseburger. The trick is to "treat" yourself on occasion when you feel like you deserve it. Make healthier choices throughout the week, and eat only until you are satisfied. Listen to your body's needs. When you have a "sweet" craving, choose similar foods that contain less fat; *in place of your fatty* snack, try choosing better options. Have a homemade oatmeal raisin cookie, angel food cake, frozen yogurt with fresh fruit, whole-wheat crackers, vegetable thin crust pizza, or a turkey burger.

Fat & Fat

Will eating fat make me fat?

Fat is an energy source that provides 9 kilocalories of energy per gram. It provides an unlimited amount of energy in the body and has an unlimited storage for it. The food pyramid guidelines suggest eating 20–35 percent of total calories as fat. There are such things as "bad" and "good" or essential fats. "Bad" fats are saturated fats and trans fats. According to the guidelines, less than 10 percent of total daily calories should be from saturated fats, which are lipids in solid form. Less than 300 mg of cholesterol is ideal. Examples of saturated fats are animal products such as butter and cheese. For reference, one egg contains approximately 215 mg of cholesterol, all of which is found in the egg yolk. Hydrogenated oils, unsaturated fats turned into saturated fats, enhance storage life in products such as many potato chips, fast-food items, and baked goods. These trans-fatty acids may raise low-density lipoproteins (LDL) cholesterol, or bad cholesterol. A high level of LDL cholesterol has been linked to increased risk of heart disease, diabetes, cancer, sleep apnea, and joint problems. This is due to the fat stored in your abdominal area beneath your organs and muscle. Abdominal fat has easier access to the blood, creating a higher risk due to many obese-linked diseases. This is why a measuring tape for your waistline is a great tool to measure your health.

Because of the detrimental effects being detected due to trans-fats, the government in some states has limited them in restaurants to a minimum of 0.5g per serving. In other words, it is easy to stay away from transfat!

On the other hand, the essential fats, Omega 3, and omega 6 fatty acids may provide healthful benefits. These monounsaturated fats may help reduce high blood pressure and protect the nervous system (nutrition for lifecycle). Good sources of omega 3s are fish such as sardines, tuna, salmon, and herring. Omega 3s and omega 6s are found in olive, canola, and fish oils as well as flaxseed, dark-green vegetables, and walnuts (droz.com). Thirty to forty percent of the recommended fat intake should be monounsaturated fats.

Polyunsaturated fats are found in sesame and vegetable oils. These are better choices than saturated also and should become 20–40 percent of total fat intake (droz.com). Here's the bottom line: eat a limited about of saturated fats (solids), avoid trans fats (many processed foods), and make mono or polyunsaturated fats (liquids) your main source of fat intake. These fats are needed to protect vital organs, to produce testosterone and estrogen, and satisfy your taste buds, leaving you feeling full. In addition, lipids are necessary to carry and help absorb fat-soluble vitamins, D, E, K, and A, to the body (ACSM).

SIMPLY PUT

Limiting your fat intake and eating balanced meals will help you achieve fat loss and minimize your health risk. There are simple ways to cut out fat when baking or cooking.

GOOD CHOICES	BAD CHOICES
Tuna (fresh or packed in water)	Fats from meats
Salmon	Fats from dairy
Olive oil	Cheese
Canola oil	Butter
	Chips
	Baked goods
	Fast foods

Protein Supplements

Do protein drinks/supplements build muscle?

As great as it would be to drink only a delicious chocolate protein shake and start seeing muscle tone in a few days, it is not realistic. Protein, the third energy source, is a nutrient that contains 4 calories/grams made up of building blocks called amino acids. It is necessary in the diet to build and maintain muscle, bone, connective tissue, organs, teeth, hair, and nails (ACSM). It is not particularly efficient in providing fuel for our bodies like carbohydrates and fat. The recommended dose of protein for the average individual is 0.8g per body weight or 10–35 percent of daily calories (ACSM).

For people looking to increase muscle mass, a recommended dose of up to 1.4–1.7g/kg of body weight may be beneficial (ACSM). The key to gaining muscle mass is eating a well-balanced meal of whole foods with an adequate amount of protein along with resistance training at least three days a week. The body is susceptible to change, and with progressive overload of weight, reps, and sets, it will adapt by building muscle tissue. Will protein supplements build muscle? No, but they can aid in doing so by helping you reach the recommended amount of protein for building tissue, in the 1.7gram/calorie range. However, if you are trying to lose weight, protein shakes might make it difficult to lose the extra pounds, since they contain calories. Excess calories are stored as fat!

The best sources of protein are lean meat and low-fat dairy. People who consume little or no animal products may need additional protein supplements. Vegetarians, particularly vegans, should supplement their diets with legumes, nuts, tofu, and raw vegetables. These are categorized as incomplete proteins because one or more amino acids are missing. In this case, a vitamins-and-mineral supplement may be beneficial. After tracking your diet, if you notice that you do not consume enough protein, consider taking a supplement.

SIMPLY PUT

Recommended amount for average adult: 0.8g/kg (i.e., 140-pound woman should consume 51 grams = 204 calories)

Recommended amount for adult wanting in increase muscle/drop weight: 1.7g/kg (i.e., 140-pound woman should consume 108 grams = 433 calories)

Protein supplements are not necessary unless you are not getting enough protein through food.

The best protein sources are lean meats.

BEST PROTEIN CHOICES

Skinless chicken	Skim milk
Turkey (white meat)	Low-fat yogurt
Beef and pork products	Low-fat cottage cheese
*Look for beef with the word loin or round in them for the leanest options.	Legumes
	Nuts and seeds
Top sirloin, bottom/top round beef, pork loin	Eggs
	Peanut butter
Bison	Raw vegetables
Venison	Tofu
Vegetable patties	

If you are short on protein sources, a protein supplement might be okay. However, whole foods are the best choice as they provide natural vitamins and minerals.

Protein & Low Carbohydrates

Is it better to eat a high- protein and low-carbohydrate diet?

In the past years, a high-protein, low-carbohydrate diet has become popular. Cutting carbohydrates means consuming more protein and typically a higher amount of saturated fats. If consumed long term, this may lead to high cholesterol, high blood pressure, and an increased risk of heart disease. Protein is broken down into amino acids, which are used for small amounts of energy or turned into fat and nitrogen. Nitrogen is excreted from the body through urine.

Excess protein can lead to an excess of ketones, which can damage the liver or kidney as well create body odor and unpleasant breath. That does not sound very appealing. Cutting carbohydrates can be dangerous if the source is restricted. A low-carbohydrate diet is dangerous because you are depriving your body of the number-one fuel source for activities as well as your brain of necessary fuel. If you are trying to lose weight, cutting out carbohydrates completely can cause decreased energy, low mental functioning, and persistent snack cravings, which are usually high in fat.

Carbohydrates are needed to reach fat stores. If weight loss is your goal, carbohydrates are necessary. High-protein diets do provide results. But the weight loss generally is temporary. The immediate weight loss is due to the loss of water weight. Glycogen requires a lot of water; when you reduce the ingestion of carbohydrates, your body burns glycogen, therefore releasing a lot of water through urination resulting in weight loss (mayoclinic.com).

When the diet is over, the weight returns

To keep off extra pounds, your diet needs to be sustained and enjoyable. Another reason this diet is popular is that you feel full. This is due to the slow digestive rates of protein and fat. Remember a good source of whole-wheat carbohydrates not only makes you feel full but gives immediate and sustained energy and has been shown to help decrease the risk of heart disease (Science Daily).

To lose weight involves commitment to changing your lifestyle beginning with the incorporation of a variety of healthy foods in moderate amounts to your diet. Diets with too many restrictions and limits create problems.

SIMPLY PUT

High-protein, low-carbohydrate diets can be dangerous to your overall health due to high ketone levels and lack of the primary fuel source for the brain.

Carbohydrates are needed to reach fat stores and help in building muscle, and without this important macronutrient, you will suffer.

High ketone levels due to high amounts of protein can lead to damaged organs if untreated.

A well-balanced diet should include a minimum of 45 percent of total calories carbohydrates and 10–15 percent protein, or 5–6 ounces a day.

The best sources of protein are:

Lean beef	Eggs
Venison	Fish
Bison	Legumes
Chicken	Tofu
Rabbit	Nuts
Turkey	Seeds

Raw vegetables are good choices for those who do not prefer animal product.

Time & Fat

Will eating past 7:00 p.m. make me fat?

If you are not hungry in the morning when you reach for breakfast, the cause might be how much you ate the night before and/or when you ate it. Does that mean that you should stop eating past 7:00 p.m.? Not necessarily, but it is a good rule of thumb to follow. At night your body and mind are winding down, decreasing your body's metabolism rate, therefore decreasing the rate in which food is digested and used for energy. The most important thing to track is the amount of calories consumed throughout the day, not so much as to when you eat them.
For example, if you ate a late lunch or worked out during dinnertime and you are very hungry after seven o'clock, by all means, do not skip food. Weight gain becomes an issue if you are eating habitually "just because" or are making irresponsible snack choices when you are still truly hungry after dinner.

A structured meal plan with three balanced meals and two healthy snacks each day will likely decrease binges late at night. However, if late night dinner dining is typical, there are particular foods that should be avoided to avoid disrupting your normal sleeping regimen and possible weight gain.

A hormone called melatonin is released naturally by the pineal glands only in the dark (abnormal psych; mood disorders). Because it effects your sleep-awake cycle, food containing this hormone will not disrupt this vital cycle. Foods containing melatonin include oats, sweet corn, and rice (doctoroz.com). Other foods that will not keep you up late are complex carbohydrates containing serotonin such as whole-wheat pasta or vegetables (doctoroz.com). Foods high in protein and fat should be avoided late at night.

SIMPLY PUT

Do not deprive yourself of your typical amount of calories because your busy schedule pushes you to eat dinner past 7:00 p.m. Choose foods listed below that do not disrupt your normal sleep-wake cycle, and do not overindulge. Eat until you are satisfied enough to sleep well. Of course, a daily eating pattern with three well-portioned, healthy meals and two snacks is best, and consuming those calories before 7:00 p.m. is a good rule of thumb to follow. At night our bodies are tired and do not digest food for use immediately like they do for our morning meal.

Best "after seven" maintenance foods: Foods marked with asterisks are best for reduction.

- Oats*
- Corn
- Rice
- Whole-wheat pasta
- Vegetables *

Alcohol

Why can't I lose weight when I drink alcohol?

Alcohol is a carbohydrate that provides energy in a form called "empty" calories because they do not provide any essential nutrients. Unlike nutrient-dense carbohydrates like whole-wheat foods, vegetables, and fruit that provide 4 calories of energy per gram, alcohol provides 7 calories/grams. It may directly promote fat storage by slowing down carbohydrate breakdown and also increase appetite. It may also cause bone weakness because alcohol takes the place of the actual nutrients needed. If consumed on a daily basis, or if one partakes in binge drinking once or twice a week, alcohol calories can add up and exceed the energy balance.

People trying to lose weight often overlook alcohol as being additive calories. On average, alcoholic drinks contain approximately 150 calories. Some mixed drinks, for example margaritas, can contain up to 500 calories in a single drink. If you consume one drink at 150 calories five days a week for an entire year, it is possible you would add eleven pounds to your waistline. If you do not consume one drink a day, how about the time you do go out and have three, five, or ten drinks? It does the same damage. For example, if you consume five drinks in one night a week for fifty-two weeks, you could be adding eight pounds to your image just from alcohol. Let's not forget the times when you binge drink and get the munchies. Late-night binging after a night of hard drinking is the ultimate recipe for disaster for one trying to get their weight on track.

Even if you are a habitual exerciser, additional calories from alcohol create extra work and set you back from reaching your goal. Not only does it affect your energy consumption, but it also affects the energy levels that determine the amount of activity you engage in the following day. This is due not only to consumption of excessive alcohol leading to "hangover" symptoms, but lack of sleep and dehydration as well.

If continued excessively for a long period, too much alcohol can lead to bone loss, an increase in cancer risk, and decrease in overall health. If weight loss is your goal, eliminating or limiting alcohol in your diet is a necessary modification. Alcohol in moderation is considered one drink a day for women and two drinks a day for men.

How much is a drink?

12 oz. of beer
4–5 oz. of wine
One mixed drink
One shot, 80-proof stiff

APPROXIMATE CALORIES IN ALCOHOL

Red wine	4–5 oz. 100 calories
White wine	4–5 oz. 100 calories
Champagne	4–5 oz. 120–130 calories
Light beer	12 oz. 95–120 calories
Regular beer	12 oz. 140 calories
Dark beer/micro	12 oz. 150–210 calories
Cosmopolitan	4 oz. 210 calories
Margarita	8 oz. 225–500 calories
Martini	3 oz. 205 calories
Long Island ice tea	5 oz. 300 calories
Gin and tonic	8 oz. 175 calories
Rum and soda	8 oz. 180 calories
Whiskey	4 oz. 200 calories

If you choose to consume alcohol, better options are wine (the dryer the better), champagne, light beer, or mixed drinks made with low-calorie mixers (water, sparkling water, diet sodas, light cranberry juice, coffee, tea). The best options would be to choose lower-calorie beers and if you are a fan of wine to make a wine spritzer using diet soda.

SIMPLY PUT

If you are trying to lose weight, do not drink alcohol. It alters your cognition. This causes you to lose control of your eating. If you must drink, drink in moderation: one drink for women and two drinks for men. Try the lower-calorie options when enjoying a beverage and do so in good company and with a designated driver if away from home.

Pasta

The same answer applies here as if you were to consume wheat. Pasta is a carbohydrate that can be converted into energy for the body's needs. However, if consumed in excessive amounts, it will be turned into fat. Favorite pasta dishes include spaghetti with marinara sauce and meatballs, lasagna, and fettuccini alfredo. It is not that pasta that is bad for you. It is often the accessories that come along with it. Also, instead of choosing white pasta, use whole-wheat pasta to reduce the fat content and sometimes calories too.

SIMPLY PUT

If you are craving pasta, enjoy it! Enjoy the dish without feeling guilty by incorporating plenty of vegetables on your plate also. To help lessen the guilt, share your serving if eating out. If eating in, use a smaller plate and have only one helping. Don't deprive yourself; just be smart about your portions.

DATA DUMP

Please forgive me for:

I forgive myself for:

P.I.E.S. Reminder

Perseverance is not a long race; it is many short races one after another."

—Walter Elliott, priest and writer

Chapter Ten

P.I.E.S & Diet Programs

Something to Think About

> "Planning is bringing the future into the present so that you can do something about it now."
>
> —Alan Lakein

Date: _____
Today, I give thanks for

Signature: _____

Why do popular diet programs work?

They have a plan; they hold you accountable to someone other than yourself, and they provide portion control, education, and behavioral modification. It's that simple.

I workout & I still can't lose weight, why?

JANE & LISA

I work out four nights or more at a local health club. There are two women in my workouts that claim they desperately want to lose weight. Both women are under forty years of age. One is six foot tall and the other is five foot one According to clinical standards, both are obese.

Jane is thirty years old, large boned, and weighs approximately 250 pounds. Lisa is thirty-nine years old, medium boned, and approximately 150 pounds.

According to the American Medical Association Standard for Women, Lisa should weigh 112 pounds and Jane should weigh 166 pounds.

The standards by Family Education for women are a bit higher, allowing Lisa to weigh between 105–136 and Jane to weigh 147–190. Lower weights represent smaller women with less muscled frames, whereas the larger numbers represent larger-boned women with more muscle size. The Army standard for Lisa should be 123–127 pounds.

Jane's should be between 173–177 pounds. For optimal health, both women's body fat standard according to Family Education for their age should range between 21–29 percent, while the army body fat standard for both women should be 32 percent.

Both Lisa and Jane come to the club and work out at least three times a week for one hour. Both participate in kickboxing and kettle bell. Both kickboxing and kettle bell instructors include ten to twenty minutes on the treadmill, elliptical, or the bicycle. Both stress that the participants should work at their optimum. Both instructors also allow each participant to determine or work to only a level at which they feel comfortable.

In my opinion, this is a mistake because it allows excuses from both the participant and the trainer. That's the last thing an individual trying to get into good physical shape needs.

Why aren't they reaching their goal?

My theory: they are too comfortable. They feel too safe. They are not risk-takers. They know how they will feel physically after a workout and are comfortable with that. So they only allow themselves to work at a minimum.

What's the buy-off?

The buy-off is they can pat themselves on the back because they worked out three or four times during the week and have not gained weight. The workout sessions provide them with a sense of security, comfort, and the opportunity to complain and make excuses for staying the same.

Why aren't Lisa and Jane losing at a minimum?

Good question. They are lying to themselves.

How are they lying to themselves?

The lying is not intentional. After all, they show up and work out. They are simply not taking into account the fact that they are not watching their caloric, sugar, fat, and carbohydrate intake.

How do I know this?

I listened, counseled, and I have seen this pattern for thirty years. What Lisa and Jane are doing is common to many people in the weight-loss game.

What exactly are they doing?

They work out. They work at a minimal pace. They do not work out on their own. They rely on others to get their job done for them. They make excuses. They say they are too busy, that they have other priorities. They make excuses.

Why?

They simply don't want it badly enough. They are not fully committed or cannot understand that what and how much they consume is either not healthy for them, has too much fat, too much sugar, too much sodium, or simply too many calories. They refuse to give up the greasy burger, the mayo, the fries, the pizza, the wine, the beer, and make a change. They are safe where they are right now. They are comfortable. To switch things up means to change something. Change is scary. We've talked about that a lot.

What are Jane and Lisa eating?

Both start out the day eating a healthy, low-fat breakfast. They then move on to lunch. Each of them has a salad with halibut. That sounds good, and it would be, if they didn't put one or two tablespoons or even a fourth cup of creamy ranch dressing on the salad. By adding that much dressing, the low-fat salad now has become a high-fat salad. They dine out for dinner at least three nights a week. Typically, they eat grilled chicken Caesar salad with creamy salad dressing, two dinner rolls with butter, and a glass of wine. Snacks throughout the day include a low-fat fiber bar, an apple with two tablespoons of peanut butter, pretzels, and diet soda. By the end of the day, their daily diary looks like this.

*Note: This daily diary is based on serving size and is estimated.

DAILY DIARY

Breakfast: 1/2 cup of oatmeal = 150 + low-fat milk = 120 calories and 2 cups of coffee with a fat free low-fat creamer = 50 calories
Subtotal = 320 calories

Snack: Fiber bar (120) calories + 1 cup of coffee with fat free, low-fat creamer (25) calories
Subtotal = 145 calories

Lunch: 4 ounces of Halibut = 200 + salad (veggies 100 calories) + 3 tbsp of creamy dressing=320
Subtotal = 620 calories

Snack: two tablespoons of peanut butter = 190 calories and small apple = 55–60 calories
Subtotal = 250 calories

Dinner: Grilled chicken Caesar salad= 390 calories + two rolls with butter = 620 one glass of wine = 120 calories

Subtotal = 1,130 calories

Snack: 1 serving of pretzels = 120 calories + diet coke = 0 calories
Subtotal = 120 calories
Approximate total caloric intake = 2,465 calories

Why is this important?

Jane and Lisa's daily caloric intake is over the 1100–1600 calories allowed on the reduction plan. Both women are not burning more calories than they are taking in. Furthermore, if we were to look more carefully at their diary, we would find the fat, sodium, and sugar intake exceeds allotted amount for their weight-reduction program.

Exercise and good nutrition are the basic essentials for staying fit. Burn what you put in, and if you want to lose, burn more. When you eat more calories than you need, your body stores the extra calories and you gain weight. When you eat fewer calories than you use, your body uses the stored calories and you lose weight. When you eat the same amount of calories as your body uses, your weight stays the same.

What does a good plan look like?

A good plan includes physical responsibility and personal accountability. A good plan provides goal-setting techniques with realistic expectations. This is essential since each individual is different with respect to education, need, and experiences. A good plan caters to the person as a whole and continually strives to reach individual needs: physically, intellectually, emotionally, and spiritually. A good plan is straightforward and does not deviate from hard work. It requires the individual to get in touch with the true problems associated with his or her eating issues. It also encourages individuals to seek help from specialists and professionals in the areas of physical, intellectual, emotional, and spiritual health so the individual can obtain his or her goals and become a healthier individual.

A good plan does not pretend to have all the answers but does work to help the individual so he or she can reach their goal or goals. A good plan is educational, economical, healthy, offers ongoing support, and is practical, safe, and sensible. It should contain at least four phases. Use these guidelines when selecting your diet program online or in a diet center.

PHASE 1: *Conditioning, break-in, or preparation phase*

This allows the body and mind a transition period from previous eating habits and food patterns or routines. This means cutting out bad sugar and replacing it with foods and vegetables, high-protein foods low in animal fat.

PHASE 2: *Reduction*

The program should include a reduction/decreased monitored caloric intake phase until you reach a healthy weight or their goal weight. This allows the client time to establish better eating habits and break bad habits. It includes a healthy eating plan that contains all food groups, requires daily exercise, provides the client with an exchange program and practical and economical eating options. It should include a variety of foods so the client does not get bored and offer resources for health and psychological issues that might arise. A healthy caloric intake for weight reduction is between 1,000 calories to 1,600 calories. This is dependent on a doctor's recommendation and individual needs. The reduction phase should encourage individuals to lose no more than three pounds a week.

PHASE 3: *Stabilization & transition*

The program should include a stabilization period or transitional period after the reduction phase so the client can be carefully monitored in order to ensure the old habits are gone and that new ones are firmly planted.

PHASE 4: *Maintenance*

It should include a maintenance or safeguard protection for at least one year. A better plan would be two years. The best plan would be a three- to five-year plan. This enables the client to continue his/her new eating habits with close monitoring while being able to express daily concerns and stressors. Ideally, they need a buddy or a sponsor they can connect with at any time for any reason. This helps to add to security and helps to provide more time for change.

The program should include behavior modification and nutritional education meetings. This helps to make the client accountable for their actions and provides them with the knowledge needed to continue a healthy lifestyle.

Why P.I.E.S.?

P.I.E.S. does what most diet clinics, weight loss centers recommend. It puts you in charge of your wellness lifestyle. It also recommends that you get help when you need it.

If you want to lose weight, you must commit to new ways of thinking and work toward developing a healthier lifestyle for yourself and your family.

Quick review before getting started

WEIGHT LOSS: INCORPORATING P.I.E.S

- *Physical*: a state of well-being. To achieve bodily wellness and maintain it once it is achieved, it is necessary to feed the body with nutritious foods, exercise it regularly, avoid harmful behaviors and substances, and protect oneself from accidents or harm.
- *Intellectual*: the ability to think and learn from life's experiences, both taught to us and experienced by us. It is a willingness to be open mindedness to new ideas and the ability to question and evaluate information with reason and logic. An individual with good intellectual skills is capable of making decisions, setting realistic goals, meeting challenges, and coming up with sensible and practical solutions to their problems.
- *Emotional*: the ability to differentiate thoughts and feelings and to communicate them reasonably and responsibly. It is the ability to interact effectively with other people in social environments. It is the capacity to develop satisfying interpersonal relationships and to fulfill social and workplace roles.

Spiritual: a belief in a higher power that gives greater significance to individual life.

SIMPLY PUT

Losing weight is not something that is going to happen overnight. Remember, you didn't put the weight on in a day or two; it took time. It took time to collect that extra baggage. It took time to realize it was even there. It is going to take time, change, hard work, and patience. Before you know it, you will be feeling more energized, more confident in you as a whole person, and feel proud of yourself each time you look in the mirror.

Losing weight means making a change, a major change in your life. A diet plan existing for only weeks or months at a time is a plan setting you up to fail once you stop the diet. Dropping pounds and keeping them off is a lifestyle change, a commitment to your health, body, and mind.

Make sure you are ready ... and make the commitment.

Educate yourself on the importance of carbohydrates, proteins, and fat by reading the material written. If you understand why you should eat certain foods and why you should minimize others, this can help with your changes. Educate. Empower. Engage.

KEY FACTORS

- Accountability
- Attitude
- Commitment
- Determination and diligence
- Patience and time
- Truth

So how do you get it done with P.I.E.S.?

P.I.E.S. teaches you to plan, and it holds you accountable. It does not allow you to use others as your excuse. You take the first step, you face your problems, and you decide to change. Want to change. Call on the P.I.E.S. original formula.

      Desire
+ Motivation
+ Commitment
+ Flexibility
+ <u>Acceptance</u>
= Change

DATA DUMP

Please forgive me for:

I forgive myself for:

P.I.E.S. Reminder

"You accomplish victory step by step, not leaps and bounds."
—Lyn St. James, race-car driver

Chapter ELEVEN

Moving Forward & Lightening the Load

Something to Think About:

"Life becomes real only when we begin to face and solve our problems. Until then we only swim in circles in a large fantasy world, which tends to make us very tired of living. Don't waste energy! Face life now!"

—Unknown Source

Date: _____
Today, I give thanks for

Signature: _____

First Step: *Cindy*

Cindy's physical and emotional desperation hit her the evening her husband rejected her sexually. It brought her to tears. The next morning her children crushed her. She wanted to give them a ride to school, but they told her they were embarrassed to be seen with her in public.

Their brutal honesty sent her to the family doctor and then to my door. When she entered my office, I could tell she was broken and desperate. As she cried and confessed her feeling of ugliness and shame, it was clear Cindy was broken-hearted. Cindy's acknowledgment of her problem was a huge accomplishment. She decided to change and wanted to create a change. She needed help. She needed to be surrounded by people who could offer encouragement and tough love when necessary. She needed to create a healthier and happier life for herself.

Cindy's next step was even bigger. It was to step on the scale in my presence. This is extremely difficult for people who have weight problems. Stepping on that scale in front of me meant her lies would be exposed. It meant facing her dirty, weighty secret. It meant no more denial.

Confronting the fact that she needed to lose more than 150 pounds was overwhelming. After determining her ideal weight, we had to frame this within a series of smaller, attainable goals, without ever losing sight of the ultimate goal.

"Take baby steps," I'd say. "One day at a time, one pound at a time. We are in this together."

Like many overweight individuals, Cindy had not been overweight as a child or young adult. As a matter of fact, as a girl she frequented the beaches of California in her teeny-weeny bikini. After moving to Oregon, she began putting on weight. Clouds and rainy days are common in Oregon, and people who move from sunshine states sometimes spiral into depression. Feeling the doom and gloom from the Oregon weather, Cindy began trying to eat her way out of depression. She missed the sunshine, she missed California, and the food became an escape, an excuse that helped fill the void.

Her children's fondness for Toll House cookies helped to fill the void. Her husband, being a meat and potatoes man, provided her with the excuse to make big meals. These realities also allowed her to use the three people she loved more than anything to justify her excuses. Baking, cooking, licking, and nibbling became a way of life.

She was eating a dozen cookies before the kids arrived home from school. After school, she would sit with them and eat two or three more cookies. Before the kids got home, she'd hide cookies so they would be available when she craved them or felt lonely or sad.

Soon she was hiding other food and eating late at night. Instead of drinking water, she drank soda and juice. Instead of eating three meals a day, she ate all day long. Her weight was out of control. Cindy didn't like looking at herself in the mirror. She found herself repulsive and would use negative self-talk when talking to herself. She convinced herself that being overweight was an unsolvable problem. She convinced herself that losing weight was impossible. She convinced herself that being obese was her destiny. She believed that food provided her with comfort and love. She believed food was an essential ingredient that helped get her through the ups and downs in her life.

In desperate need of help, Cindy felt ashamed and overwhelmed. After weeks, months, and years of abusing herself, it was time to take action. This meant facing truths about herself, wanting to lose weight, coming to the office six days a week, stepping on the scale, having sessions with her weight-loss counselor, using reprogramming techniques/strategies, and setting goals. Below are some mental reprogramming statements Cindy used to help reach her ultimate weight loss goal of 121 pounds.

Before I left Oregon, Cindy became my secretary/receptionist. She became a true inspiration. In the spring of 1983, her husband received a transfer with United States Postal Service. With her new image came confidence. Being an inspiration to others, the corporate office and I made it our mission to help Cindy create a new career by looking for opportunities with the company. Our employment searches paid off, and she was offered a position with the company in Arizona. Cindy created her change. She lost her weight, changed her hair color, and moved to another state, a sunny state.

EXERCISE: *Are you ready to create change?*

Are you content living in complacency? Yes or No

Are you ready to change? Yes or No

Are you ready to be accountable for your own life? Yes or No

List one to three things you can commit to change today.

Physically:

Intellectually:

Emotionally:

Spiritually:

French Fries & Getting Real

I was overweight and needed to do something about it. I was in the eighth grade. My body was changing daily, and I believed I could eat anything I wanted without gaining weight. I was a scrawny child. I even wore suspenders. I honestly believed I would never gain weight. After all, every time I saw Susan she was eating fries and burgers. She remained slim and beautiful.

This misconception caused me to put on ten to fifteen extra pounds that my small, short frame most definitely did not need. I couldn't see it until one day somebody took a snapshot. Thanks to the art of photography, I was forced to look at that chubby girl and admit to myself I didn't like what I saw. I needed to do something about it. Deep down I knew I was overweight because I could see my fat thighs and butt every time I got dressed, tried on a pair of pants, or saw my cute little sister. As much as I tried to deny it, I couldn't; it haunted me daily. I overheard a conversation between my grandmother and my mother about how chubby I was getting. I felt ashamed and humiliated. Even though the words hurt, they weren't even close to the disgust I felt for myself every time I looked in the mirror. However, those words uttered in private conversation were what motivated me to take action.

This chubby young lady read every magazine and article she could get her hands on and went on a yogurt and apple diet. I did not deviate from my eating ritual until I lost my weight. Because the magazines stressed the importance of exercise, I began riding my bike daily, putting in six to ten miles a day while working three jobs. Working and focusing on riding the bike kept my mind off my stomach and provided me the ability to lose my unwanted fat.

As I reflect back, I am very much aware of how unhealthy all this was for me, but I also realize what motivated me to slim down. The fact is sometimes we need reality to slap us in the face to get moving.

So get real with yourself and face the fact that the only way to a healthier body is to eat sensibly and exercise.

This period in my life taught me to forever be aware of health decisions. To this day, I maintain an excellent body composition and am in great physical, mental, and spiritual condition for a woman my age.

Perhaps that young adolescent led me down this path. I don't know why it took me so long to see it, but it did. All I know is when you eat right and exercise daily, you feel good about yourself and this leads to a healthier and happier you.

Are you eating too many French fries?

EXERCISE: *List the Truth & Action*

List the truths you need to face about yourself. Take one action or step toward each truth. Record your action adjacent from the truth.

Truth: Are you overweight? Yes or No

Truth: Why?

>Mindless eating
>Emotional eating
>Too much overindulgence
>Too much fast food
>Don't care
>No exercise
>Other _____

Truth: Do you want to lose weight? Yes or No

Truth: Do you want to eat healthier? Yes or No

Truth: Do you know what you weigh? Yes or No

Truth: Do you know your measurements? Yes or No

Are you ready to learn the plan? Yes or No

Let's Get Started

Action Step: Step on the scale and enlist help.

Action Step: Write your weight down. I weigh _____ pounds.

Action Step: Write your measurements down.

> Neck:
> Bust:
> Wrist:
> Arms:
> Waist:
> Hips:
> Thighs:
> Calves:
> Ankle:

Action Step: Clean up your environment.

Action Step: Donate unopened fatty or high-caloric food to a food bank.

Action Step: Organize your space and gather your tools.

- Scale
- Tape measure

- Notebook/journal to track exercise progress and daily food intake (example in workbook) or join online (mypyramid.gov)
- Measuring cups/spoons
- Calorie Counter (mypyramid.gov) or purchase a food scale
- Healthful Recipes (see recommendations, mayoclinic.com) reusable Ziploc containers (prepare ahead!)

Action Step: Enlist your support team: friends, family, doctor, fitness coach, etc. These are going to be your go-to people.

Action Step: Set up your walking plan: call a buddy, set up a time to walk, walk by yourself, or walk your dog. Write the time on your calendar, Blackberry, or day planner. Commit!

Action Step: Take a thirty-minute walk. If you must, do fifteen minutes in the morning and fifteen minutes in the evening. Do more minutes if you can.

Action Step: Go to the grocery store. Purchase only foods on the grocery list. (A suggested list is found near the end of the book.)

Action Step: Prepare your foods for the week (Sunday)

Cook six or seven skinless chicken breasts or turkey breasts (grill, broil, or bake) seasoned to taste. While chicken/turkey is cooking, clean and chop vegetables and put in Ziploc bags or containers. Make a salad with lettuce, spinach, and vegetables of choice; toss. Use the rest of veggies for snacking or making a stir-fry with chicken.

Wash your fruits and make them visible and available. Get a fruit bowl and place it on your countertop with apples, oranges, bananas, pears, lemons, limes, etc. With fruits needing refrigeration (strawberries, grapes, cantaloupe, and melons) prepare them by washing and cutting so they are readily available!

While you're at it, prepare low-cal salad dressings, dipping sauces, homemade breakfast meals (granola bars, muffins).

Action Step: Learn to modify recipes and make simple substitutions

HEALTHY COOKING TIPS

Replace high-fat beef with lean beef, ground turkey, or rabbit. Rinse your meat after you brown it.

Replace sour cream with low-fat, nonfat sour cream or low-fat, nonfat yogurt such as Hidden Valley Ranch vegetable dip.

Replace creamy dressings with vinaigrette and oil dressings (best option for dressings).

Modify creamy dressings with low-calorie salad dressings or low-calorie mayonnaise. (Read the labels: look for low-sugar, low-fat dressings or learn to make your own.) Replace whole egg with two egg whites or egg substitutes. Replace lard with cooking spray (i.e., Pam), canola, vegetable, or olive oil. Fresh seasonings are best, but dried are fine.

Milkshake fan? Replace with a fruit smoothie using frozen or fresh fruit, low-fat, nonfat milk, or yogurt. Rule of thumb: no more than 1/8 teaspoon of salt per serving. If a recipe makes four servings, use no more than 1/2 tsp of salt (1/8 x 4). Replace microwave popcorn with air popped or 100-calorie microwave bags

Replace sugar with sugar substitutes (i.e., Agave, Equal, honey, Stevia, Sugar Twin, Sweet'n Low, Splenda).

Action Step: Join a gym. Set a time to go to the gym every day. Stick with it. Set a time to take a thirty-minute walk. Stick with it. Come rain or shine. Get some fresh air.

Did you take your walk today? Yes or No

Truth: Did you get on the scale? Yes or No

Truth: If you did, why? If you didn't, why not?

Truth: What did you weigh?

Truth: What are your measurements?

Action Steps: Walk thirty minutes. Go to the gym and work out.

Action Step: Learn the Reduction Plan

Water: 6 to 8 glasses of water a day or 1/2 your weight in ounces (nothing replaces water)

Dairy: 1 to 2 servings of 1% low fat, skim, soy, nonfat dairy servings

Fruit: 2 to 3 servings per day (one should come from the citrus family, i.e., 1/2 grapefruit, one should come from an apple).

Vegetables: 3 to 4 servings per day (only 1 from the starchy group, i.e., corn, potato, squash, try to eat these sparingly).

Breads, cereals, grains: 1 to 2 servings per day (read the labels carefully, i.e., 6 Triscuits, 2 Wasa Bread, 1 bagel, 1 slice of Natures Pride Bread, 1/2 cup of oats, 3.4 cups of Special K, etc.

Fats: 1 to 2 servings daily (no butter, no margarine) the fats come from those on your list, i.e., olive oil.

Action Step: Prepare your *Daily Food and Activity Diary*. Copy mine if you like. You should set it up for seven days at the least.

DAILY FOOD & ACTIVITY DIARY

Name:

Date:

Goal Weight:

Today's Weight:

Today's Mood:

Today's Promise:

Breakfast:

Midmorning Snack:

Lunch:

Afternoon Snack:

Dinner:

Evening Snack:

Exercise Activity:

Mood:

Accomplishments:

Smart Tips

TIME OF DAY

Eat at the same time every day, and plan your meals and menus.
Plan your snacks and the time of day in which you will eat them.
If you work, pencil in your meal times, and be strict about it.

ENVIRONMENT

Avoid places that give you problems.
Surround yourself with positive and supportive people.
Eat before leaving the house to avoid temptation.
Take your own food, diet drinks, and water bottle to social events and parties if necessary.
Take inventory of your home environment so you can plan and stay on the program.

EATING-OUT TIPS

Try to avoid fast-food restaurants.
If you must eat at fast-food restaurants, educate yourself. It really is best to stay away simply because the smell of oily burgers and fries could be too tempting. However, if you must eat at a fast-food restaurant, choose wisely.
Smart choices are salads without chips or a bowl, wraps without dressing (you add your own).
Avoid large orders. If you give into temptation, order small and share. Savor the taste.
Order a dinner salad and water. Bring your own salad dressing.

Use vinegar and oil.

Ask that your dressing be served on the side.

Ask the waiter or waitress not to bring bread and butter to your table.

Order only from the low-calorie menu.

Avoid reading the dessert list.

Drink water.

Be assertive.

Problem foods: don't buy them; don't eat them.

Eat low-calorie snack food.

Drink water first.

Drink a diet soda or sugar-free drink first.

Chew sugar-free gum.

Do not sample food while preparing.

Learn to modify and substitute.

FOOD INTAKE

Measure all portions.

If you want more, reach for the veggies.

Eat on a smaller plate.

Practice leaving some food on your plate.

Do not skip meals!

BUYING & STORING

Never shop on an empty stomach.

Take your weight-reduction list with you, and only buy what is on your list.

Avoid aisles with tempting foods.

Go for color—usually the darker, the better.

COOKING & ENTERTAINING

Always broil, bake, or grill.
Learn to modify and substitute ingredients.
Try new, low-calorie recipes.
Make low-calorie recipes for company.
Prepare veggie trays and fruit trays for company.
Make meals a social event.
Make your meals colorful.

LOCATION, POSITION, ACTIVITY:

Eat only at designated eating places.
Do not watch television or read while eating.
Sit while you eat.
Take at least twenty minutes to eat a meal.
Watch what you eat while traveling.

EMOTIONS & THINKING:

- Do relaxation and self-talk. Express yourself.
- Exercise.
- Stay away from negative people.
- Write in your journal or diary.

Suggested Plan

"Today I shall savor each moment and appreciate my beauty."
—LPS

Day 1

Water Count:

Breakfast:

Raisin oatmeal
Low-fat, fat free or soymilk
Coffee or tea
Water
Vitamin supplement(s)

Morning Snack:

1 apple, sliced
Coffee or tea
Water

Lunch:

Tossed salad with tuna fish
Sugar-free beverage
Water

Afternoon Snack:

Cottage cheese with pear
Water

Dinner:

Steak
Baked potato (fat-free or mock sour cream) (no butter)
Asparagus
Sugar-free pudding (made with low-fat, skim, or soy milk)
Water

Day 2

Water Count:

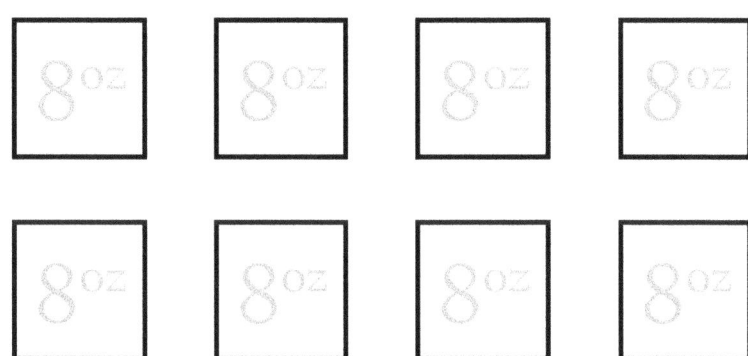

"Today I shall expect to succeed, therefore I shall."

—LPS

Breakfast:

Pita pocket egg sandwich
Coffee or tea
Water
Vitamin supplement(s)

Morning Snack:

1 apple, sliced
Coffee or tea
Water

Lunch:

French dip sandwich
Carrots and celery sticks and cherry tomatoes
Sugar-free beverage
Water

Afternoon Snack:

Sugar-free yogurt
Coffee or tea
Water

Dinner:

Fresh fish
Cole slaw
Bailey's garden pasta
Angel food cake with berries

Day 3

Water Count:

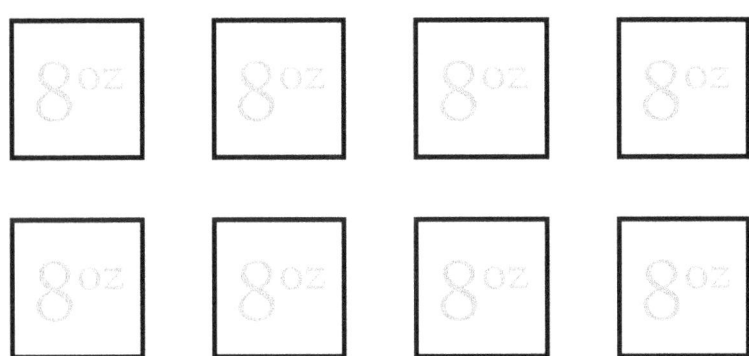

"Today I shall greet myself and others with a smile."
—LPS

Breakfast:

1/2 grapefruit
1 bran or banana raisin muffin
Coffee or tea
Water
Vitamin supplement(s)

Snack:

1 apple, sliced
Coffee or tea
Water

Lunch:

Spinach salad
Sugar-free beverage
Water

Afternoon Snack:

Nutty, fruity cottage cheese snack
Water

Dinner:

Chicken breast
Corn
Dinner salad (with fat-free dressing, lemon, or vinegar)
Quick sherbet or store bought sugar free
Water

Maintenance Plans

College Student

- Rise early
- Groom
- Drink a glass of water
- Eat breakfast and have black coffee with splash of milk or low-fat flavored cream.
- Go to school and work
- Eat lunch (30 minutes)
- Back school and work
- Afternoon snack
- Work out at a local gym (cardio and weights).
- Relax at home.
- Cook and eat dinner.
- Chores
- Relax
- Go to bed early

MEALS

Breakfast

- Oatmeal and banana with glass of water and black coffee with a splash of milk

Lunch (variety)

- Peanut butter and jelly sandwich on whole wheat and an apple, water
- Turkey sandwich on whole wheat with lettuce and tomato and yogurt, water
- Tuna and bean pita with a glass of orange juice
- Salad with vegetables I have on hand and sliced turkey or ham with vinaigrette dressing and a piece of whole-wheat toast, water
- Homemade leftover soup

Snack choices (typically 30–45 minutes before my workout)

- Half a banana and 90-calorie chewy bar (I eat the other half of banana after my workout)
- Apple with 1 tablespoon of peanut butter
- Oatmeal
- Handful of cashews or almonds if my day off of workout
- 1 serving whole-wheat chips and salsa (not usually before a workout! This is my treat!)

Dinner (variety)

- Chicken and rice or whole-wheat pasta with a variety of vegetables
- I love homemade soup, so any broth based and/or vegetable soup
- Chili made with lean meat
- 2 lean beef or chicken tacos in whole-wheat tortilla with lettuce, very little cheese, and salsa

WORKOUT ROUTINE

Monday, Wednesday, Friday

- Bike
- Alternating time of 45 min or 60 min and inclusion of intervals
- Leg workout (15–30 min)
- Lunges
- Adductors/abductors
- Leg flexors and extensors
- Stretch (5–10 min)

Tuesday, Thursday, Saturday

- Run for 30 or 45 min and sometimes include 5–10 min of rowing before beginning arm workout
- Either at 8-min mile speed or do speed intervals
- Arm workout with inclusion of jump-roping in between reps and/or abdominal workout
- Triceps—either dips or overhead raises
- Push-ups
- Shoulder press
- Lap pull-downs
- Pull-ups
- Abdominal workout
- Variety of abdominal workouts for 15 min
- Stretch (5–10 min)
- Sunday—rest; sometimes I may go for a walk or do a light cardio on the elliptical

Off-Season Body Builder

MEALS

Monday, Tuesday, Wednesday (Low carb—50g)

- Meal 1—1/2 C oat bran, 1.5 scoop whey protein, 1 T almond butter, 2 tsp fish oil
- Meal 2—5 oz. lean ground turkey, green beans
- Meal 3—5 oz. chicken, broccoli with hummus, 1/3 C brown rice (second carb meal right after workout)
- Meal 4—5 oz. fish, 1 T almond butter, green beans
- Meal 5—5 oz. lean cut steak, asparagus
- Meal 6—6–8 egg whites, 1 T almond butter

Thursday (High carb—150g)

- Meal 1—2/3 C oat bran, 1.5 scoop whey protein, 1 T almond butter, 2 tsp fish oil
- Meal 2—1/2 C brown rice, 5 oz. fish
- Meal 3—1/2 C brown rice, 5 oz. lean ground turkey
- Meal 4—5 oz. chicken, broccoli with hummus
- Meal 5—1 C brown rice, 5 oz. chicken, 1 T almond butter (fourth carb meal right after workout)
- Meal 6—5 oz. lean cut steak, green beans

Friday (med carb—100g)

- Meal 1—1/2 C oat bran, 1.5 scoop whey protein, 1 T almond butter, 2 tsp. fish oil
- Meal 2—1/3 C brown rice, 5 oz. chicken

- Meal 3—5 oz. fish, broccoli with hummus
- Meal 4—5 oz. lean ground turkey, green beans
- Meal 5—2/3 C brown rice, 5 oz. fish, 1 T almond butter (third carb meal right after workout)
- Meal 6—5 oz. lean cut steak, green beans

Weekends

- Cheat without indulging.
- Go out for one or two meals.

Workout Routine

- Mon—chest/biceps
- Tues—back/rear deltoids
- Wed—off
- Thurs—legs
- Friday—off
- Saturday—shoulders/triceps
- Cardio (30–45 min) and abs 3 times a week

Zumba Fitness® Instructor's Lifestyle

MEALS

Breakfast

- Take two Laminine supplement capsules w/ 8oz of water
- Wait 30 minutes till eating anything

- Make a 8 oz. cup of coffee w/ bowl of cereal and whole wheat toast
- Cup of berries or banana

Mid-Snack

- Walnuts and banana
- 24 oz. of Brita filter water

Lunch

- Leafy green spinach mix salad w/ olive oil and croutons
- Either cup of soup or chicken salad sandwich
- Walnuts & piece of fruit

Afternoon Snack

- 12 oz of Brita filtered water
- One serving of crackers (read label)

Dinner

- Chocolate milk (only after Zumba workouts)
- String cheese
- Bowl of cereal and whole wheat toast
- 12 oz. of Brita Filtered water

*Bedtime take 2 capsules of Laminine 30 minutes before sleeping.

ZUMBA FITNESS® CLASS SCHEDULE

Monday

- Zumba® Class (1 hr. cardio + Latin dance rhythms)

Tuesday

- Day off from Zumba®
- Walk around the block for 45 minutes

Wednesday

- Zumba® Class (1hr. cardio)

Thursday

- Zumba® Class (1 hr. cardio)

Friday

- Day off from Zumba®
- Walk around the block for 45 minutes

Saturday

- Walk to the park and around the block (1 hr.)

Sunday

- Day of rest

Mother & Career Person

- Pray, for self and others
- Write daily intentions on paper.
- Read daily inspirational quotes and a story.
- Write daily goals and intentions.
- Plan the day
- Prioritize.
- Take time for self.
- Take time for others.
- Groom
- Work (try to work with positive people).
- Eat healthy

MEALS

- 6–8 glasses of water daily
- No sugared beverages during the week

Breakfast

- A sugar-free whole-grain cereal with fruit.
- Usually oatmeal with raisins in the winter.
- Coffee-black, sometimes a fat-free creamer
- Yogurt with 1/4 cup of granola and fruits in season
- Coffee

Lunch

- Soup
- Chicken noodle—low sodium, low fat
- Minestrone—low sodium, low fat
- Salad with low cal or no cal dressings

- Sandwich with 3 ounces of turkey or tuna on whole grain bread, whole-grain flat bread, pita, or low-fat wrap loaded with vegetables.

Dinner

- Skinned chicken breast
- Salad or side dish (rice or pasta ½ cup)
- No dessert
- Tacos made with lean beef or chicken
- Limited cheese (Yes, I do buy yellow cheese and use it for tacos. However, I use very little. I load it with vegetables. Sometimes I opt for just having a salad with very a small portion of crumbled whole-grain taco chips. I usually have salsa for my dressing. I seldom use sour cream. If I do I take about a tablespoon. I usually will only have one taco.)
- Grilled burger, lean or sirloin, with bun and veggies
- Salad
- Beverage

Weekends

- Go out to dinner and remain mindful
- No desserts
- One or two glasses of wine

WORKOUT ROUTINE

Monday & Wednesday

- Kettle bell and elliptical or treadmill (1 hour workout)
- Elliptical or treadmill

- Change the incline and miles per hour. (This keeps the body guessing.)
- Warm up (3.8 mph or 4mph with an incline of 3% for 4–5 minutes.
- Increase 3% incline every 30 seconds until you reach 15.
- Decrease 3% every 30 seconds always maintaining 4–5 set mph.
- Recover at 3% incline for 3 minutes at 4–5 mph.
- Increase incline 3% every minute up to 15 incline.
- Decrease incline 3% every minute until you reach 3% incline.
- Cool down at 3.8 mph or 4mph for 5 minutes.
- If you want to really shake things up, run. amp up 5.5 mph or higher for a minute. Do this throughout the routine.
- When applying this to the elliptical increase tension and incline.
- Make sure you have your tension and incline the same.
- Constantly speeding up and down.
- Cool down 4–5 minutes.

Tuesday & Thursday

- Kick boxes and elliptical or treadmill (1 hour workout)
- Walk when I can and when I want.
- Use stairs instead of elevators.
- Pilates

Friday, Saturday, Sunday

- 30-60 minutes walk (outside)
- Go to the club
- Hike a mountain

Note: When I want to drop weight, I amp up my walks to about two hours a day.

Mother, Grandmother, & Business Owner

- Wake up at 3:20 a.m.
- Work by 4:00 a.m.
- 4:15 a.m. Coffee (black)
- Water 32 oz.
- 6:00 a.m. breakfast (Oatmeal or yogurt)
- 9:30 a.m. (piece of fruit or granola bar)
- Water 32 oz.
- 12:00 (noon) off work

Monday–Friday 1:00 p.m. workout

- Legs
- 25 minutes on the elliptical
- 75 leg reps with exercise ball (medicine ball)
- 40 leg lifts
- Core
- 40 sit-ups

Monday, Wednesday, Friday

- Arms
- 10 lbs 15 overhead and in front with squats

Tuesday & Thursday

- 45-minutes workout (whatever makes me happy)
- Total gym (arm and stomach)
- Wii games balance and walking
- Yoga or other exercises

Note: *When the weather is nice, I enjoy walking and hiking. I am fortunate to live near a river and often walk the banks of the river. I try to walk 45 minutes or more a day. In the winter, I enjoy cross-country skiing with my husband and friends. We generally will do two to three miles. Following this regime, I have lost 16.5 pounds in twelve weeks.*

Mother, Teacher

Monday-Friday

- 6:00 a.m. wake up
- shower and groom
- 6:30 a.m. breakfast and quiet time (1/2 grapefruit, 1 sugar-free/low-fat bran muffin, coffee black)
- 7:00 a.m. get kids up and ready for school
- 7:45 a.m. kids off to school, and off to work
- 8:00 a.m. workday begins (no break until noon); I keep water and coffee at my desk.
- 12:00 noon (tuna salad with vinegar for dressing, four crackers coffee and water)
- 12:40 p.m. back in the classroom
- 3:05 p.m. school dismissed. Get a diet soda and pretzels (low sodium); work at my desk until 4:30 p.m. or later.
- 5:00 p.m. prepare dinner (skinned chicken—grilled, broccoli, fruit salad, and water)
- 6:00 p.m. walk with a friend for one hour
- 7:00 p.m. sliced apple

Retiree

MEALS

- Low-fat, low-cal program (like the Betty Crocker Health Series Cook Books)

WORKOUT ROUTINE

Monday, Wednesday, Friday

- 30 minutes swimming or soggy jogging

Tuesday & Thursday

- 3 miles on the recumbant bike
- treadmill with a bit of an incline for cardio

DATA DUMP

Please forgive me for:

I forgive myself for:

P.I.E.S. Reminder

"A busy mind and body rests well."

—LPS

Chapter Twelve

Wrap It Up

Something to Think About:

> "Good for the body is the work of the body, and good for the soul is the work of the soul, and good for either is the work of the other."
>
> —Henry David Thoreau

Date: _____
Today, I give thanks for

Signature: _____

Seven Days of Recipes

Breakfast suggestions

RAISIN OATMEAL

- Oatmeal serving size for one with low-fat, fat-free, or soy milk (top with raisins if desired or sweeten with cinnamon sugar substitute)
- Cup of coffee or tea
- Glass of water with vitamin supplement(s)

PITA POCKET EGG SANDWICH & MIXED BERRIES

- 4 egg whites or 1/2 cup of egg substitute
- 1 cup of low-fat cheddar cheese, shredded
- 1/2 mini pita pocket
- 3/4 cup blueberries
- 1 teaspoon olive oil
- 1 cup strawberries

Preparation: Add olive oil to skillet and preheat. Combine egg whites or egg substitute with spices. Pour into skillet and cook to individual liking. Sprinkle on cheese. Remove and load into pita pocket. Place on a breakfast plate and surround with mixed berries.

- Cup of coffee or tea
- Glass of water with vitamin supplement(s)

CINNAMON OATMEAL WITH SLIVERED ALMONDS

- 3/4 cup low-fat cottage choose with 3 teaspoons of slivered almonds; add cinnamon to taste

Preparation: Add oatmeal to 1/2 cup of water in a bowl, and cook in microwave oven for 2 minutes and cook again for 10 seconds to heat cottage cheese. Sprinkle on cinnamon and top with slivered almonds.

- Cup of coffee or tea
- Glass of water with vitamin supplement(s)

BLUEBERRY BUTTERMILK PANCAKES

- 1 cup buttermilk
- 1 egg + 1 egg white
- 1 tablespoon oil
- 1 cup flour
- 1 tablespoon baking powder
- 1/2 teaspoon baking soda
- 1/2 teaspoon salt
- 1 cup blueberries, fresh or frozen

Preparation: Beat together buttermilk, eggs, and oil. Mix dry ingredients and add milk mixture, blending well. Stir blueberries in gently (if frozen no need to thaw.) Cook on medium-hot with non-stick griddle until brown on both sides and firm to touch. Makes twelve four-inch pancakes. Serving size three. Top with sugar-free syrup.

- Cup of coffee or tea
- Glass of water
- Vitamin supplement(s)
- Poached eggs
- 2 poached eggs
- 1 slice of toast
- 1 orange (peeled, sliced, or wedged)
- Cup of coffee or tea
- Glass of water with vitamin supplement(s)

LOW-FAT EGG & SAUSAGE BREAKFAST

- 1 English muffin (toasted)
- 1/4 cup of Egg Scrambler
- Lean sausage (Turkey)
- 1 slice of fat-free cheese

Preparation: Toast muffin. Cook sausage according to directions on package. Prepare egg scrambler omelet style and place patty on muffin, add cheese, zap in microwave or melt from the heat of the pan, and sandwich together.

- Cup of coffee or tea
- Glass of water with vitamin supplement(s)

SHREDDED WHEAT

- 1 cup of shredded wheat with low-fat, skim, or soy milk
- 1 banana (your choice slice and add to cereal)
- Cup of coffee or tea
- Glass of water with vitamin supplement(s)

Lunch Suggestions

TOSSED SALAD WITH TUNA FISH

- 2 ounces albacore tuna, water packed and drained
- 2 macadamia nuts, chopped
- 1/2 apple (medium cored and cubed)
- 1/3 cup mandarin orange, canned in water and drained

Dressing:

- 1 teaspoon mayonnaise (low fat)
- 1 teaspoon lemon juice (fresh or bottled)

Preparation: Combine lettuce, apple cubes, and mandarin oranges, tuna, and macadamia nuts in a large salad bowl. Blend mayonnaise, yogurt, and lemon juice in a small cup to create dressing. Pour dressing over the salad and toss.

- Sugar free beverage and water

SPINACH SALAD

- 2 cups of fresh spinach
- 2 hard-boiled eggs (peeled and sliced)
- 1 cucumber (sliced)
- 2 carrots
- 2 tablespoon of Bacos
- 1 green onion
- 1 tomato sliced

Preparation: Buy prepackaged to make life easier. Put spinach into serving bowl; add cucumber slices, carrots, onion, and eggs; toss, and garnish with Bacos and tomato. For a salad dressing, use your favorite low fat, or use vinegar or lemon. Be sure to measure your dressing.

- Sugar-free beverage and water

FRENCH DIP SANDWICH

- 1/2 cup beef broth
- 1/2 cup of water
- 1 cup red wine
- 1 tablespoon Worcestershire sauce

- 1 pound flank steak
- Garlic powder
- Onion powder
- Salt and pepper to taste
- 4 Long crusty French rolls
- Mustard-mayo cream

Preparation: Heat together broth, water, wine, and Worcestershire sauce to make the dipping broth. Season the steak with garlic powder, onion powder, salt, and pepper to taste; broil until rare or to taste. Toast French rolls by splitting them lengthwise and placing them cut side down in a hot, nonstick frying pan. Spread Mustard-Mayo Cream on one half of each roll, pile on the meat, cover with the second half of the roll, and serve along with a small cup of dipping broth. Serves four. Yield at one.

Mustard-Mayo Cream:

- Mix equal parts of low-fat or fat-free sour cream and Dijon mustard
- 1 cup of fruit in season (fresh is best, if canned sugar-free)
- Sugar-free beverage and water

BARLEY SOUP

- 4 cups chicken broth
- 1/2 pearl barley
- 1/4 dried basil
- 1/2 chopped celery
- 1/2 chopped carrots
- 1 cup chopped mushrooms

Preparation: Simmer broth, barley, basil, celery, and carrots together until barley is tender (about one hour). Add mushrooms, and simmer 15 minutes. Adjust salt. Serves four. Yield at 1 serving.

- 1 cup of fruit in season (fresh is best, if canned sugar-free)
- Sugar-free beverage and water

STIR FRY TURKEY OR CHICKEN WITH VEGGIES

- 3 to 3 1/2 ounces skinless chicken or turkey breast
- 1 to 1 1/2 cups zucchini
- 1 teaspoon olive oil
- 1 cup green beans
- 1 1/4 cups tomatoes chopped

Preparation: Cut turkey or chicken breast into strips, and stir-fry in the olive oil until done. Remove turkey breast with the veggies, mix, and serve hot.

- Sugar-free beverage and water
- 1 cup of fruit in season (fresh is best, if canned sugar-free)

Dinner Entrée Suggestions

FRESH FISH

- 5 oz. fresh fish

Preparation: Heat 1/4 cup water and 1 teaspoon vinegar almost to boiling in a small nonstick pan. Add fish, reduce heat, and simmer 5 minutes. Lift fish carefully from the water and place under pre-heated broiler for 2 minutes each side or until lightly brown and flakes with a fork.

TOMATO CRAB CUPS

- 1 small fresh tomato
- 4 oz. cooked crab or shrimp

Preparation: Cut off stem end of tomato and scoop out the seeds and pulp. Mash seeds and pulp with crab or shrimp meat. Fill tomato with crab and serve chilled.

GRILLED OR BROILED STEAK

- 1 pound of steak
- 2 tablespoons soy sauce
- 2 teaspoons honey or sugar substitute
- 1/4 teaspoon hot pepper sauce
- 1/4 teaspoon garlic powder

Preparation: Mix marinade ingredients well; pour over steak placed in plastic bag. Let stand 4–24 hours in the refrigerator, turning often to distribute marinade. When ready to cook, remove from marinade and place over coals or broil until done to your liking. Serves four.

BARBECUED STEAK

- 1 pound of steak
- 1/4 cup wine vinegar
- 1/2 teaspoon onion powder
- 2 teaspoons Worcestershire sauce
- 1/2 teaspoon dried thyme
- 1/4 teaspoon garlic powder
- 1/8 teaspoon hot pepper sauce

Preparation: Mix marinade ingredients well; pour over the steak placed in plastic bag.

Let stand 4–24 hours in the refrigerator, turning often to distribute marinade, and place over hot coal or under broiler until done to liking. Serves four.

APPLE POT ROAST

- 2 pounds lean, boneless meat
- 1 teaspoon oil
- 6 small onions
- 5 carrots cut in thirds
- 1/2 cup sliced celery
- 1 bay leaf
- 1 cup apple juice
- 1 cup beef broth or wine

Preparation. Heat oil in Dutch oven. Add beef; brown well on all sides. Add remaining ingredients; cover, and place in 300-degree oven for 1 1/2–2 hours or until tender. Serves eight.

EASY OVEN BAKED STEW

- 1 pound lean beef, cut into 1-inch cubes
- 2 medium onions
- 2 large carrots
- 4 celery stalks
- 8 large mushrooms
- 1 teaspoon oil
- 1 teaspoon salt
- 1/8 teaspoon garlic powder
- 1 bay leaf
- 2 tablespoons Worcestershire sauce
- 2 cups water

Preparation: Brown beef in hot nonstick skillet. Remove from pan. Cut onions in quarters, carrots and celery in 3-inch lengths, and leave mushrooms whole. Add oil to skillet and brown vegetables briefly. Arrange meat and vegetables in deep ovenproof casserole, sprinkle with salt and garlic powder, add bay leaf. Bake at 300 degrees for 1 1/2 hours or until very tender. More water may be added. Serves four.

Lasting Advice from P.I.E.S.

P.I.E.S. is a time of self-discovery. The best way to discover who you are is to get involved. Do as much as you can. Don't overextend. Don't be afraid to join clubs or organizations. Step out of your comfort zone and meet new people. You say, "hi" first. Don't be afraid. Chances are if you want to meet them, they probably want to meet you.

Volunteer, give blood, help with the food bank, help register voters; just do whatever you can. You never know; your blood might be the blood chosen to save a life. How cool is that? The food you helped collect is probably helping some family that doesn't have food in their cupboard. You helped give them a meal they might not have had. How cool is that? Help someone register to vote; his or her vote might be the one that made the difference. How cool is that? Some of the best times are those you spend helping others. Some of the best experiences are those that you receive through serving others. These are the times and experiences you will carry with you for a lifetime. This is your life, so you may as well do it right and make it count.

When you make a mistake, don't make excuses or look for someone to blame. Own your mistakes. That's how you learn. Take your stumbles in stride. Don't let them keep you down; if you allow yourself to stay down, you might find yourself in a deep, dark hole. And this is when you become vulnerable and make very poor choices. Don't let bad influences cloud your journey. Stay clear!

Don't let others stop you from enjoying your life. Avoid the toxic people in your life. If someone tries to get you to do something you know is wrong, walk away. Have your safe people in place. They are the ones you can call if you're about to do something stupid, such as drive drunk or eat a carton of ice cream. They are the ones you call when you just need a sounding board. Know your "go-to" people; the people you can count on when you're in a jam.   Remember, just because you can count on them doesn't mean they are always going to say what you want to hear; most of the time they'll tell you the opposite. They're the only ones brave enough, who truly care and love you. They are the ones who will help you relight your torch when it burns out. They are the ones who will remind you that happiness is yours to possess.

FINAL DATA DUMP

Please forgive me for:

I forgive myself for:

Today is the first day of the rest of my life. From today forward I will:

P.I.E.S. Reminder

"Water helps to flush and wash the impurities of the body away."
- LPS

LPS Weight Loss Grocery List

Shopping made easy! Just check and go!

    Note: *Foods marked by an asterisk are best for stabilization and maintenance. They are to be used sparingly while on reduction.*

PROTEINS

Beef (lean)	Herring	Scallops
Bison	Octopus	Sea bass
Chicken Breasts	Mussel	Shark
Chicken Livers	Ocean perch	Shrimp
Catfish	Orange Roughy	Sole
Crab	Oyster	Smelt
Lobster	Perch Pike	Swordfish
Deer (not at store)	Pollock	Sturgeon
Elk (not at store)	Pork	Trout
Eggs	Rabbit	Tuna (fresh or water pack)
Flatfish	Red Snapper	Tofu
Flounder	Sablefish	Turkey
Haddock	Salmon	
Halibut	Sardines	

Note: *If you are on the reduction plan, you are allowed two 3 ½ servings of protein a day.*

VEGETABLES

Alfalfa sprouts	Chicory	Pickles
Artichoke	Chinese cabbage	*Potatoes
Arugula	Collards	Snow peas
Asparagus	*Corn (starchy)	Shallots
*Avocados (high fat)	Cucumber	Snow peas
Bamboo shoots	Dandelion green	Spinach
Bean sprout	Endive	*Squash (starchy)
Beet greens	Eggplant Green beans	Tomatoes
Bok choy	Kohlrabi	Turnips
Broccoli	Lettuce	Turnip greens
Cabbage	Mushrooms	Watercress
Carrots	Mustard greens	Wax beans
Cauliflower	Okra	Yard long beans
Celery	Onion (all kinds)	Yellow beans
Chard	Peppers (all kinds)	Zucchini

Note: If you are on the reduction program, you are allowed four servings per day.

FRUITS

Apples	Elderberry	Mandarins
Apricots	Gooseberry	Nectarines
Asian pears	Mulberry	Oranges
*Bananas (high fat)	Raspberry	Papaya
Blackberry	Strawberry	Passion fruit
Blueberry	Fig	Peaches
Boysenberry	Grapefruit Grapes	Pears
Cantaloupe	Guava	Persimmons
Casaba	Honeydew	Pineapple
Cherries	Kiwi	Plums
Crabapple	Kumquat	Pomegranate
Cranberry	Lemon	Star fruit
Crenshaw	Lime	Tangerines
Currant	Mangoes	

Note: If you are on the reduction program, you are allowed two to three fruits a day.

SEASONINGS & SPICES

- Allspice
- Basil (variety)
- Bay Leaves
- Bouillon cubes (beef, chicken, vegetable)
- Bon Appetite
- Butter seasoning (salt free)
- Cayenne pepper
- Chinese five spices
- Chives
- Chili powder
- Cilantro
- Cinnamon
- Cumin
- Curry
- Dijon mustard
- Dill weed
- Dry mustard
- Garlic powder
- Garlic salt
- Ground coriander
- Ground ginger
- Hot sauce
- Italian seasonings
- Lemon juice
- Lime juice
- Low-sodium salt
- Minced garlic
- Mrs. Dash (salt-free)
- Oils (Flaxseed)
- Onion soup mix
- Oregano
- Packaged dry chili
- Paprika
- Parsley flakes
- Pepper (black and white)
- Pumpkin spices
- Vinegars
- Mint
- Rosemary
- Sage
- Sesame seeds
- Soy sauce (low sodium)
- Tarragon
- Thyme
- Whole peppercorns
- Worcestershire sauce

BEVERAGES

- Coffee
- Sugar-free cranberry
- Crystal Light
- Crystal Light Fitness (Water)
- Kellogg's Special K
- Protein water mix
- Diet soda
- Herbal teas
- Tea
- *V-8 juice (tomatoes and veggie)
- Water (#1)

Note: *You need 6–8 glasses of water a day or half your weight in ounces (i.e., if you weigh 130 pounds, you need 65 ounces a day.) Do not substitute your water for other beverages.*

BREADS & CEREALS

Ak-Mak crackers	Melba Toast	Rye crisp
Bran cereal (Brand Buds, All Bran)	Multigrain	Saltines (no salt)
	Norwegian flatbread	Shredded wheat
Finn crisp crackers	Oatmeal (Raw)	Wasa crisp crackers
Flat bread	Pita bread	Whole wheat
Hollywood (brown)	Puffed rice	Zoom
Italian breadsticks		

Note: Breads, cereals, pasta, rice, and grains are to be eaten sparingly. You must read the labels very carefully. If you are on the reduction program, you are allowed two to three servings per day. Remember corn, potatoes, and squash are considered starches, so include them here.

PASTA, GRAINS, RICE

(Whole grain best pick)	Millet	Popcorn (Air popped or 100-calorie packs)
Brown rice	Pasta shells	
Corn meal	Penne	Spaghetti
Linguine	Pilaf	White rice

DAIRY

Buttermilk (low-fat, reduced fat, or nonfat)	Ice cream (low-fat, sugar free, nonfat)
Cottage cheese (low fat, 1%, 2%, or nonfat)	Milk (1%, 2%, or skim)
	Rice milk
Creamers (Half and Half, Coffeemate fat free, International Delight low fat, fat free)	Soy milk
	Sour cream (low fat, nonfat)
	Yogurt (plain, unsweetened, low-fat, nonfat)
Dry milk (nonfat)	

Note: If on the reduction program, you are allowed two servings of dairy per day. Read the labels carefully.

OILS

Extra Virgin Olive Oil
Flaxseed Oil
Nonstick cooking spray
Seasoned oils (example chili oil)

Note: *If you are on the reduction program, you are allowed two servings of fat per day. So stick with nonstick cooking spray when cooking, and use oils for dressings and special ingredients. Remember avocados and bananas are high in fat.*

SUBSTITUTE SUGARS

Agave
Equal
Honey
Splenda
Stevia
Sugar Twin

DESSERTS

Jell-O
Jell-O pudding (low fat, nonfat, no sugar)
Ice cream (low fat, sugar free, nonfat)
Popsicles (sugar free)

Note: *You are allowed one of these treats a day.*

SALAD DRESSINGS (Vinaigrette based)

Vinaigrette dressing (homemade best)
Kraft Organic Balsamic (low fat, low sugar, sugar free)
Kraft Balsamic Vinaigrette (low fat, low sugar, sugar free)
Kraft Raspberry Hazelnut Vinaigrette (low fat, low sugar, sugar free)
Kraft Raspberry Vinaigrette (low fat, low sugar, sugar free)
Lighthouse Raspberry Walnut (low fat, low sugar, sugar free)
French dressing (low fat, low sugar, sugar free)

CANNED FOODS

- Kidney beans
- Black beans
- Crushed tomatoes
- Fruits and veggies (no sugar or salt)
- Tomato paste
- Stewed tomatoes
- Sugar-free fruits
- Low-sodium beef stalk
- Low-sodium chicken stalk
- Low-sodium vegetable stalk
- Tomato-based sauces (low sodium)

SOUPS (low sodium, no MSG preferred, Progresso or Campbell)

- Chicken noodle
- Minestrone
- Vegetable
- Tomato

CHEESE (white/best choice)

- Feta
- Mozzarella (low fat, non fat)
- Parmesan
- Ricotta (part skim)
- String cheese (low fat, non fat)
- Swiss

Bibliography

ACSM's Resource Manual for Guidelines for Exercise Testing and Prescription. 6th ed. Baltimore, MD: Lippincott Williams and Wilkins, 2006. Print.

Alcamo, I., Edward, Ph.D. *Fundamentals of Microbiology*, Fourth Edition. California: Benjamin/Cummings, 1994.

Bailey, Covert. *Fit or Fat*. Boston. Houghton Mifflin Company, 1978.

Bailey, Covert and Bishop, Lea. *Target Recipes for Fit or Fat Folks*. 1984.

Bailey, Gerry. "Yo-Yo Syndrome Sometimes Harmful" *Argus Newspaper*. Portland. Date unknown.

Berger, Kathleen S. and Thompson, Ross, A. *The Developing Person Through Childhood and Adolescence*, Third Edition. New York: Worth Publishers, 1986.

Brown, Judith, E. Ph.D. M.P.H., R.D., Issaacs, Janet S., Ph. D.R. D., Mutaugh, Ph.D. R.D., Sharbaugh, Carolyn, M.S., R.D., Stang, Jamie, Ph.D, M.P.H., R.D., and Woolridge, M.S., R.D., L.D. *Nutrition Through the Life Cycle*, Third Edition. Belmount: Thomson Wadsworth, 2008.

Birkinshaw, Elsye. *Think Slim—Be Slim*. Santa Barbara: Woodbridge Press Publishing Company. 1981.

Blanchard, Kenneth, Ph.D. and Tammyson, Spencer, M.D. *The One Minute Manager*. New York: Candle Communications, 1981.

Carnegie, Dale. *How to Win Friends and Influence People*. USA: Simon and Schuster. 1937.

Carnegie, Dale. *Stop Worrying and Start Living*. USA: Simon and Schuster. 1984.

Carnegie, Dale. *Principles of The Golden Book, How to Win Friends and Influence People*. Dale Carnegie and Associates: 2006.

Cassidy, Catherine. *Figure Maintenance*. Mountain View: Anderson World, Inc. California. 1983.

Comer, Ronald, J. *Fundamentals of Abnormal Psychology*, Fifth Edition. New York: 2008.

Coonrandt, Charles, A., and Nelson, Lee. *The Game of Work*. Salt Lake City: Liberty Press, 1984.

Darconte, Lorraine. *Lessons of Success*. New York: MJF Books, 2001.

Diet Center Inc. "The Yo-Yo Syndrome" Newsletter. Rexburg: Ferguson and Associates, 1981.

Diet Center Inc. "Be a Goal Getter!" Newsletter. Rexburg: Ferguson and Associates. 1982.

Diet Center Inc. "The Mind's Eye." Newsletter. Rexburg: Ferguson and Associates. 1983.

Diet Center Inc. "Eating Disorders Epidemic Proportions." Rexburg: March 1984.

Doe, Tammy, Father. *The Golden Book of the Spiritual Side*. Indianapolis: the SMT Guild, Inc., 1979.

Egan, Kieran, *Educational Development*, New York: Oxford University Press, 1979.

Evans, Gail, *She Wins You Win*. New York: Gotham Books, 2003.

Evans, Gail. *Play Like a Man, Win Like a Woman*. New York: Broadway Books. 2000.

Ferguson, Sybil. Diet Center, *It's a Natural Cookbook*. Diet Center Inc. 1983.

Field, Tim, *Bully Insight*, Didcott: Success Unlimited. 1996.

Frank, Otto. *Anne Frank: The Diary of a Young Girl*, New York: Bantam Books, 1993.

Fink, Heather, H., Burgoon, Lisa, A., and Mikesky, Alan E. *Practical Applications in Sports Nutrition*, Second Edition. Sudbury: Jones and Bartlett Publishers, 2009.

Goleman, Daniel, *Emotional Intelligence*. New York: Bantam Books, 2005.

Good House Keeping presents, Dwight D. Eisenhower's Favorite, Prose, and Prayers. Unknown: Hearst Corp. 1957.

Hubbard, Ron L., Fall Symposium 2003. Portland: Hollander Consultants, 2000.

Heavin, Gary and Manley, Jane. *Permanent Results without Permanent Dieting the Curves for Women Weight Loss Method Fourth Edition*. Waco: 2001.

Krauser, Herriette, A., Ph.D. *Write It Down, Make It Happen*. New York: Fireside Schuster, 2000.

Kubany, Edward, S., Ph. D., Mc Gaig, Mari, A., MSCP and Laconsay, Janet, R., MA, *Healing the Trauma of Domestic Violence A Workbook for Women*. Oakland: New Harbinger Publications, Inc. 2004.

Lefkowits, Tammy, Ph.D. and McDuff, David R., M.D. *Mental Toughness Training Manual for Baseball/Softball Players*. Date unknown.

Lucado, Max, *Grace for the Moment. Nashville:* J. Countryman, 2000.

Mayo Clinic Staff. Bulimia nervosa. http://www.mayoclinic.com/health/bulimia/DS00607. November 11, 2009.

Mc Graw, Jay, *Life Strategies for Teens*. New York: Free Press Inc. 2003.

Mc Graw, Phillip, C. Ph.D. *Self Matters, Creating Your Life from the Inside Out*. New York: Free Press Inc, 2001.

Mc Graw, Phillip, C., Ph.D. *Self Matters Companion*. New York: Free Press, Inc. 2002.

Milazzo, Vickie L. RN., MSN, JD. *Inside Every Woman. New Jersey:* Tammy Wiley and Sons, Inc. Hoboken, 2006.

Miss Montana Staff. 1990 *Miss Montana Pageant Contestant Workshop Booklet*, Miss Montana/Miss America, Billings: 1990.

"Neighbors Name Alice Cobb District Deputy" Livingston; Livingston Enterprise, August 22, 1968.

O'Leary, Tim. *Warriors, Workers, Whiners and Weasels Understanding and Using the Four Personality Types to Your Advantage.* Katonah: Xephor, 2006.

Parker, Valerie and Gates, Ronda, *The Lowfat Lifestyle.* Lake Oswego: 1984.

Parsons, Doris. *Journal from Friends and Family.* Livingston: 1998.

Parsons, Doris. *Notes and Papers.* Livingston: 1975.

Parsons, Lorna. *Notes and Papers.* Billings: 1977.

Parsons, Lorna. *Lorna's Co-counseling Journal,* Billings: 1977.

Parsons, Lorna. *Notes and Papers.* Billings: 1978.

Parsons, Sherry. *Letter to Lorna.* Livingston: 1998.

Pangrazi, Robert, P. and Dauer, Victor, P. *Dynamic Physical Education for Elementary School Children,* Tenth Edition, New York: Macmillian, Inc. 1992.

Parese, Steve, Ed.D., *Workin' It Out Revised 2005 Trainer's Manual,* Denver Workforce Imitative the Piton Foundation, Danbury: SBP Consulting Inc. 2005.

Popkin, Michael, H., Ph.D. *Active Parenting Now,* Atlanta: Active Parenting Publishers, 2002.

Rimrock Foundation Staff. *Eating Disorders.* http://www.rimrock.org/treat/eating.shtml. November 2, 2009.

Robbins, Anthony. *Get the Edge.* San Diego: The Anthony Robbins Company, 2000.

Robbins, Anthony, *Personal Power.* San Diego: The Anthony Robbins Company, 1996.

Ronnow, Karin. "A Montana Life." Bozeman: Bozeman Daily Chronicle, April 8, 1997.

"Saturday Night Fever" Livingston: Livingston Enterprise, April 2, 1979.

Sebranek, Patrick, Meyers, Verne, Kemper, Dave. *Write Source 2000.* Massachusetts: Houghton Mifflin Company, Wilmington, 1995.

Simons, Janet, A., Irwin, Donald and Drinnien, Beverly A. *Maslow's Hierarchy of Needs—The Search for Understanding*. New York: West Publishing Company, 1987.

Smt., Jolly, Ray, Dr. *Mental Toughness*. Bangalore: Karnataka State Hockey Association, April 16, 2003.

Sumner, Mona, L., *Eating Disorders: The Female Experience*. Deaconess Health Information. Billings: Rimrock Publications. 1986.

Tarascio, Sara, *Hope Springs Eternal*, New Rochelle: Salesians Missions, 1978.

Timonium, MD. *Life Styles, The Medifast Program of Patient Support*. Unknown: The Nutrition Institute of Maryland, Inc. 1989.

"My Struggle with Anorexia and Bulimia, I'm Not Cured I'm Still Fighting" *Shape Magazine*, September 1983.

Bulimia,Binge,Eating,RespondtoTalkTherapy. http://www.medical-newstoday.com/printerfriendlynews.php?=166653. November 11, 2009.

Stremcha, Lorna, *Confidential Interviews Regarding Eating Disorders*. Havre: 2009.

Stremcha, Lorna, *Gratitude Journal*. Havre: 2003.

Stremcha, Lorna. Workshop Notes and Papers: *Fitness, Nutrition and You*, 1990.

Stremcha, Lorna. *Resolutions! LPS Weight Loss Grocery List, Shopping made easy! Just Check and go!* LPS Productions: 2003.

Stremcha, Lorna. *Resolutions! Plan Your Life! Love Your Life! Live Your Life!* Havre: LPS Productions: 2003.

Walker, Sharon. "Happy Birthday Alice!" Livingston: Park County Weekly, March 19, 1997.

Wooden, Tammy, and Jamison. Steve, *Wooden on Leadership*. New York: Mc Grawl Hill, 2005.

Young, Adena. Battling Anorexia: The Story of Karen Carpenter. http://atdpweb.soe.Berkeley.edu/quest/MindandBody/Carpenter.html. November 18, 2009.•

www.ingramcontent.com/pod-product-compliance
Lightning Source LLC
Chambersburg PA
CBHW071301110426
42743CB00042B/1131